W9-CFL-579

FAITHFUL FINANCES 101

FAITHFUL FINANCES 101

From the Poverty of Fear and Greed to the Riches of Spiritual Investing

 confused

Gary Moore

Foreword by
Sir John Templeton

TEMPLETON FOUNDATION PRESS
PHILADELPHIA AND LONDON

To hearts, souls, and minds over money

Templeton Foundation Press
Five Radnor Corporate Center, Suite 120
100 Matsonford Road
Radnor, Pennsylvania 19087
www.templetonpress.org

© 2003 by Gary Moore

All rights reserved. No part of this book may be used or reproduced, stored in a retrieval system, or transmitted in any form or by any means, electronic, mechanical, photocopying, recording, or otherwise, without the written permission of Templeton Foundation Press.

Scripture quotations from the *Good News Bible: The Bible in Today's English Version*, copyright © 1976, by the American Bible Society, are used by permission. All rights reserved.

Designed and typeset by Gopa & Ted2, Inc.
Printed by Sheridan Books

Library of Congress Cataloging-in-Publication Data

Moore, Gary D.
    Faithful finances 101 : from the poverty of fear and greed to the riches of spiritual investing / Gary Moore ; foreword by John M. Templeton.
      p. cm.
Includes bibliographical references and index.
    ISBN 1-932031-30-8 (alk. paper)
    1. Wealth—Religious aspects—Christianity. 2. Finance, Personal—Religious aspects—Christianity. I. Title.
BR115.W4 M66 2003
241'f.68—dc21

                                            2003001843

Printed in the United States of America

03 04 05 06 07   10 9 8 7 6 5 4 3 2 1

CONTENTS

ABOUT THE AUTHOR

DURING THE EARLY 1980s, Gary Moore wrote an article for *The New York Times* newspaper group about why the Dow Jones might triple from the 1000 level to the 3000 level despite the predictions of best-selling, doom-and-gloom authors. During the late 1980s, he wrote what *Christianity Today* called "the first book outlining a comprehensive scriptural basis for an evangelical embrace of ethical investing." During the early 1990s, he wrote a book about why the federal debt was political illusion rather than a major economic concern. At the request of the Church of England, he then taught biblical economics to the leadership of Uganda in order to demonstrate that Christianity can enrich this life at least as abundantly as Islamic economics. During the late 1990s, his writings explained why Y2K was media hype but stock market speculation and questionable corporate ethics were the true dangers to our finances.

Mr. Moore has a degree in political science from the University of Kentucky and was a senior vice president of investments at Paine Webber before thinking of seminary in the late 1980s. He was surprised to discover that seminary would not teach anything about wealth management. So he began informal study of the subject and founded his own investment firm as "counsel to ethical and spiritual investors." He has since advised some of America's well-known ministries, churches, banks, and individual investors while authoring five other books about integrating religion and spirituality with personal financial management and political economy.

He is or has been a trustee of the Crystal Cathedral, serving as chair of its audit and endowment committees; a trustee of Messiah College, serving on its endowment committee; a board member of the John Templeton Foundation; a board member of the Joy Leadership Center; the board treasurer of Opportunity International, a microenterprise organization that makes two-hundred-dollar loans for the creation of jobs in the Third World; a board advisor to Jack Kemp and Bill Bennett's Empower America; the lay leader of both a Lutheran and an Episcopal church; and a financial commentator for UPI International Radio and the Skylight Radio Network.

He lives in Sarasota, Florida, with his wife Sherry and son Garrett. You can access more of his thinking at www.financialseminary.org.

FOREWORD

THOSE WHO DO GOOD DO WELL. This ancient maxim applies to clergy as well as to all other careers and businesses.

This fact is found often in the Bible and the scriptures of other religions that have survived by helping humans to become more productive. Every life work is a ministry if focused on doing good.

Evidences are that investing in shares of companies that produce products or services that are beneficial will be more profitable in the long-run than investing in enterprises which may be harmful.

The Bible words that express these facts are, "It is more blessed to give than to receive."

Of course, depending on the gifts that God has given to you, there are many ways in which you can give. You need to know how to discern which of those various ways is right for you.

That is why my friend Gary Moore, with whom I've worked for many years attempting to better integrate faith, political-economy, and personal finance, shares the many other biblical concepts found in this book. I trust that it will be a source of rich blessings to you.

Sir John Templeton
Founder of the Templeton Mutual Funds
and the Templeton Prize

PREFACE

THE WALL STREET JOURNAL has shared a lot of wisdom during the twenty-five years I have helped people and institutions with their finances. But none of their articles has been as potentially enriching as the *Journal's* sentiment that the Bible should not only be the most purchased book in the West but the most read as well. As the last millennium was coming to a close, the paper said: "There are plenty of secular reasons to read the Bible. It may be the most important text in Western history. It's an essential part of our Western heritage and has inspired more composers, architects and artists—from Michaelangelo to Dali—than any other book. It is also a literary masterpiece, with stories and characters that still resonate today" ("A New Look for the Good Book," 12/23/99).

The *Journal* didn't mention it but the Bible is, or should be, just as "essential" a part of our economy as our arts, or even of the politics that have preoccupied many American Christians during the past two decades. Lady Margaret Thatcher, the former prime minister of Great Britain, has said: "The moral foundations of a society do not extend only to its political system; they must extend to its economic system as well. Capitalism is not an amoral system based on selfishness, greed and exploitation. It is a moral system based on a biblical ethic."

Yet that system does not produce the abundant life that we all desire when the ethic is confined to a lofty "macro" level, on a national or international scale. It must reach down to the "micro" level, to our personal finances, if we are to change the world. As Tony Campolo, professor emeritus of sociology at Eastern University in Saint Davids, Pennsylvania, put it in *Christianity Today*, "The political system does not control what happens in society. The structure of society is more controlled by economic forces than by political forces. If you want to change society, don't bother getting elected. Go to the stockholders' meetings" ("The Positive Prophet," January 2003).

That is why the Bible has a lot to say about money—about how we should think about it, how we should earn it, and what we should do with it. The main purpose of this book is to bring those biblical teachings to light so that those who desire to surrender 100 percent of their financial lives to God— and not just give 10 percent of their incomes to the church—can better think about how God wants them to do so.

As we enter our new millennium, I believe followers of Christ have not just an ongoing responsibility to be faithful in the area of finances but a historic opportunity to shape a better world. As to our responsibility, the Bible tells us that to whom much is given, much will be required. And the truth is that *anyone blessed with the average American income ranks among the top 1 percent of wage earners in human history.* Having *any* excess wealth in an IRA, mutual fund, and so on to steward places such people among the "rich" to whom the Bible refers. That's a blessing, but a huge responsibility.

As to our historic opportunity, it is doubtful that anyone can remember when Americans have been as sensitive as we are today to how religion, however true or false, can influence our finances for better or worse. We must handle this opportunity with great care. Political commentator Cal Thomas' December 4, 2002 column in the *Lexington Herald-Tribune* was titled: "Moderates must clean Islam's house." I agree that might enrich our world. But this book is essentially a plea for moderation in the West as well. If I had to cite one true danger to your finances in the immediate future it is that very conservative Christian leaders in the West will turn Islam into the giant in the promised land that they imagined the Desert Storm conflict of the early 1990s, the federal debt of the mid 1990s and the Y2K problem of the late 1990s to be. During the early 1970s, I trained as an Army officer to fight an ideologically charged enemy doing the will of a tiny state. They didn't mind using guerilla tactics on our Army in their land. Even after 9/11, I doubt that most Americans can imagine the horrors of fighting a theologically inspired enemy supposedly doing the will of God; one that doesn't mind using terrorist tactics on our civilians at home.

Please understand that we are *not* typically going to be discussing the nature of the Deity, Christ, Muhammad, and so on, which can rightly arouse our deepest passions. We will be exploring far more mundane matters, matters that are subject to the apostle Paul's counsel for "moderation in all things."

Unfortunately, the typical believers in our mainline, Baptist, and Catholic churches have not had much help from leaders in the quest toward spiritual maturity in the area of finances. Worse, much of the most popular economic counsel emanating from the evangelical media has been rather extreme. As will be explored in this book's early chapters, some media celebrities have promoted a kind of prosperity gospel that justifies for Christians the lowest forms of materialism. Meanwhile, other popular and influential evangelical authors and speakers—based on end-times scare tactics and highly questionable economic advice—have done their share to distort and suppress what the Bible has to say about finances, and divert us from true issues.

If you don't spend much time listening to evangelical broadcasts, you may be unaware of these leader's teachings and their influence, both direct and indirect. So I will discuss them by name. That has made about one-half of my friends who have reviewed this manuscript uncomfortable. Having worked in the Christian media for over a decade, I know only too well that we live in an age when Christian publications and broadcasts can openly name Christian leaders from President Clinton to Ken Lay, the chairman of Enron, to liberal Episcopal Bishop John Spong, who have fallen short; yet it's still taboo to discuss how our media leaders might have done so, particularly in the area of money. As we will see, that is most contrary to every biblical ethic this side of "take the log out of your own eye." As attested by Jesus' cleansing of the Temple, the first step toward developing a faithful approach to money, indeed the kingdom, is to recognize that we have *all* fallen short in this challenging area of life.

The second step is to put money in its proper place. That is far easier said than done in modern America. I took a step in this direction in 1990 after spending more than a decade on Wall Street, reaching the position of senior vice president of investments with Paine Webber. The tiniest amount of faith—what the Bible calls the size of a mustard seed—made it possible for me to give up my title, my pension, and my corner office. I moved my practice into my home, and in return got to watch my newborn son grow up. That has been more spiritually enriching to me than all the financial bonuses and stock options I discarded upon leaving a major investment firm.

I know it was the right decision for me. For when I was thinking of seminary, my denomination's psychologist told me I could barely see male images in inkblots. Even without knowing anything about my youth, he explained that this meant my father must have been among the ranks of those entrepreneurial absentee fathers so common in America. The psychologist knew his trade. For I can tell that story in a group of ten "successful" businessmen today and nine will typically identify with it, usually by shedding a few tears. I now firmly believe that allocating a generous amount of those assets we call time and talent to your children is one aspect of being "faithful" that can help you to achieve the abundant life.

In setting forth my other ideas and perspectives on what it means to be faithful in our finances, broadly defined, I am committed to steering clear of three extremes commonly found in books purporting to offer economic advice. First, I will not fearfully predict a poorer third millennium, believing that such a prediction would only help to create a less abundant future given the biblical principle that "as a man (or a nation) thinketh, so he (or it) will become." Second, I will not guarantee that in order to grow richer, you need only use a few selected passages of the Bible as your foolproof investment guide. And third, I will not insist that you must don sackcloth and ashes (i.e., impoverish yourself) in order to be a faithful steward.

Instead, the soul of this book will help you to visualize the abundant future that our most gracious God has promised to both "the just and the unjust," and then help you to invest love and care toward the goal of making this abundant life a reality for all. While I believe investing that love may possibly enrich you financially, I also believe that God's definition of abundance has less to do with material things than even many religious leaders proclaim these days ... though more than other leaders may believe.

This book is also, at heart, a plea for economic and theological humility. Be assured that virtually every study ever done affirms the need for more of that humility. We need to have open minds and hearts as we explore how the biblical ethic that "God is love" must shape our every thought, speech, and act as part of the process of making the economic and financial teachings of the Judeo-Christian Scriptures understandable and relevant, whether we are laity or clergy, believer or nonbeliever.

For example, if you're a typical Westerner, you're probably already thinking or feeling that the biblical ethic that God is love is an altruistic sentiment that will leave you financially poorer. But the following words from my friend, the legendary mutual fund manager Sir John Templeton, reflect both a more holistic understanding of abundance and a biblical ethic permeated by love:

> The concept that you have a life in business and a separate life spiritually is false. The two go hand in hand. If you have a spiritual life it should show in your business. The way you work with your colleagues, the way you try to help your customers, the way you treat your competitors. All those things have to be founded on love, have to be founded on giving rather than getting. And if you do that, your business will prosper. So my advice to a school of business management is to teach the business manager to give unlimited love, and he or she will be more successful.

In Jeremiah 29:11, God is recorded as saying, "I know the plans I have for you, plans to prosper you and not to harm you, plans to give you hope and a future." Jesus himself said that he came that we might have life and have it more abundantly. With this in mind, my greatest hope in writing this book is that it might create a more genuinely abundant life for you and your neighbors, for the glory of God, by putting money in its proper place and by making your financial affairs more simple, more ethical, and more prudent. If you deem my efforts successful, I invite you to share this book with your friends at your church, ministry, college, or business, perhaps by forming a spiritual investment club or business club.

Obviously, I have written this book because I feel I have something to say, something to offer. But let the record show that I make no claims to have any direct access to God's plan for managing our increasingly complicated world. Unlike some who offer economic advice based on the Bible, I do not consider my views inerrant or infallible. I am not a prophet. I aspire only to be a life-long student of God's laws and grace. In more reflective moments, I often wonder if I'm even a decent disciple. And in more spiritual moments, I acknowledge that I am the ultimate "beggar before God." But I also know with all my heart and soul that I'm loved anyway, and that love compels me to continue my struggle toward God's perfection.

I have studied the Bible, politics, and economics for some fifty years. About all that I've concluded is that almost any economy would work pretty well if the hearts, minds, and souls of humanity were simply in love with

God and with neighbor as self. As the many quotes in this book attest, I see my vocation as a spiritual financial counselor as simply being a messenger from those possible prophets who may know how such love might manifest itself in what Dr. Peter Drucker refers to in his book of the same title as our new "post-capitalist society."

In other words, after praying for humility—and like most Christians I'm always most proud of my humility—I listen carefully to those who may sit nearer to our Creator on today's mountaintop. My goal—if what they say sounds like a modern echo of the biblical prophets—is to share their ideas with people who are busy at work in the valley below.

Are those ideas guaranteed to put you in the *Forbes* list of the four hundred richest people in America? No. But I can assure you that while *Forbes* may never mention my name again, this once anxious soul is slowly becoming the "richest" man on earth.

ACKNOWLEDGMENTS

THIS BOOK is indebted to those faithful economists, money managers, management experts, and rare economic theologians whose views are too seldom shared in religious circles—particularly not by those televangelists and radio commentators increasingly utilizing mass communications to enrich, or impoverish, lives around our world both spiritually and financially. Those truly thoughtful leaders of national or global stature who have enriched my life and thinking include but are not limited to, in possible order of influence:

John Templeton, Peter Drucker, Mother Teresa, Robert Bartley, Robert Schuller, Michael Novak, Chuck Colson, Peter Berger, Henri Nouwen, Justo Gonzalez, Irving Kristol, Robert Wuthnow, Milton Friedman, Richard John Neuhaus, Robert Sirico, Thomas Merton, Doug Meeks, Francis Schaeffer, Douglas John Hall, Bruce Birch, and Bruce Howard, professor of economics at Wheaton College.

While reviewing this manuscript, my friend Lu Dunbar, a fellow student of stewardship matters, noted the lack of influence by female theologians on my thinking. You should understand that women from my mother, Kathryn, to authors such as Gertrude Himmelfarb and theologians such as Ellen Charry have greatly influenced my thinking. Yet while acknowledging the writings and work of Amy Domini on the subject of ethical investing—which is related to but on a different plane than spiritual investing—neither Lu nor I could name a woman who has done significant economic work of a spiritual or religious nature. That is most unfortunate as it may indicate that the patriarchal nature of Wall Street is rivaled only by the patriarchal nature of the church. It is even more unfortunate because I believe women will most probably play the dominant role in creating a more prudent and ethical economy. For while our philanthropy maintains its feminine, life-giving, and nurturing characteristics, our investment capital has drifted to its masculine side. In a sense, this book explains why, even with investment capital, the Bible teaches that there is no male or female in Christ Jesus (Galatians 3:28). (As this manuscript is going to press, I have begun to read *Church on Sunday; Work on Monday*, which was co-authored by Laura Nash at the Harvard Business School. Ironically it may be one of the very most important theological books of this new century as it explores how the church has defaulted to the secular "spirituality and business" movement of Deepak Chopra, and so on.)

I am also particularly grateful to the wise counsel of the Reverend Dr. Luder Whitlock, the recently retired president of Reformed Theological Seminary; the Reverend Dr. John Santosuosso, professor of history and political science at Florida Southern College; Dr. Tom Seel, an investment officer at the Presbyterian Foundation and certified financial planner who has authored a book about sacred music; Mike Ritchie, a development officer at the University of Kentucky and international president of the Gideons; and Mary Naber, a fellow student of this discipline, Merrill Lynch financial consultant in the Los Angeles area, and financial author who has a dual degree in religion and economics from Harvard University. Each of you is a source of wisdom as I struggle with my own integration of faith and finances, as well as a source of encouragement as I struggle to help others do so. You are blessed by God.

Finally, join me in thanking my editors. It is only by the friendship, encouragement, and patience of Joanna Hill and Laura Barrett that you have access to what is inside my heart, soul, and mind. Yet as an act of most gracious stewardship, Randy Frame has saved you considerable time scanning material that was far more important to me than to you, which is the most popular temptation but greatest cardinal sin of us authors!

FAITHFUL FINANCES 101

INTRODUCTION

"I'm suspicious of preaching that is not biblically based, but I'm also suspicious of preaching that's biblically confined. If one doesn't get out of
the Bible and into people's lives, I think one has missed it."

Lee Strobel, Christian minister and author

P ERHAPS INDICATING that we in the West cannot give for some good but
invest for some harm, Gandhi expressed the ancient and Eastern worldviews by saying:

> One man cannot do right in one department of life whilst he is occupied in
> doing wrong in any other department. Life is one indivisible whole. . . . I do
> not believe that the spiritual law works on a field of its own. On the contrary,
> it expresses itself only through the ordinary activities of life. It thus affects the
> economic, the social and the political fields. . . . I claim that human mind or
> human society is not divided into watertight compartments called social,
> political and religious. All act and react upon one another.

Western theologians know that should also be the modern Christian
worldview. Writes *Christianity Today* on April 26, 1999: "For Christians, the
integration of faith into all areas of life rests on Christ's vision for his church
and the world. Faithful believers may not bracket off from God any part of
their world, however resistant it may be to godly influence."

In contrast with these expressions of healthy spirituality, contemporary
religious beliefs in the West are largely disconnected from the areas of life
they are intended to inform. Dr. Bryant Myers of World Vision has written
in his book entitled *Walking With The Poor*:

> As the foundational paradigm shift of the Enlightenment has worked itself
> out in Western culture, one of its most enduring features has been the
> assumption that we can consider the physical and spiritual realms as separate

and distinct from one another . . . Sadly, this is not just a problem for Western folk. This dichotomy, or absolute separation, is a central tenet of what
some call modernity, and modernity is rapidly becoming a dominant over-
lay on the world's cultures. Modernity is deeply embedded in the modern
economic system. . . . This framework of separated areas of life is also deeply
embedded in the Christian Church, in its theology and in the daily life of its
people. On Sunday morning or during our devotional or prayer life, we operate in the spiritual realm. The rest of the week, and in our professional lives,
we operate in the physical realm, and hence, unwitting act like functional
atheists.

That is particularly true in the area of our personal finances, which is the
focus of this book. For example, some people who tithe faithfully to the
church seem totally unaware of how scriptural teaching should influence
other aspects of their financial lives, including investing. So when *The Wall
Street Journal* surveyed America's leading Christian financial planners, it concluded their advice appeared "worldly" since their counsel was "little different" from secular planners and they used the "same investments." Hence,
when we unwittingly fail to *integrate* our faith into investing as well as into
our giving, the world may see us as lacking *integrity* from Monday to Saturday. As Scott Rodin puts it in *Stewards in the Kingdom*: "Until we are willing
to face the reality of this second kingdom and move to expose it and renounce
it as an alien and counterfeit edifice, our otherwise good and well-meaning
books, programs, courses and sermons on stewardship will never make it
inside the walls of our worldly kingdom. No actual transformation will ever
take place. We will not raise up godly stewards for the work of the kingdom
of God. And the church will continue unwittingly to lend credence and context for this two-kingdom reality."
At the root of the problem—indeed at the root of most problems—can be
found a lack of spiritual depth concerning the hold money has on us.
Addressing the Philippians, Paul prayed "that your love may abound more
and more in knowledge and *depth of insight*, so that you may be able to discern what is best and may be pure and blameless until the day of Christ"
(Philippians 1:9–10, emphasis added). But in our age, while an increasing
number of American Christians have been "evangelized" as far as being able

to cite the Four Spiritual Laws or the two verses of the so-called prayer of Jabez, a much lower percentage are being discipled more deeply in biblical spirituality. A *Christianity Today* feature article entitled "The Greatest Story Never Read" described a surprising lack of biblical depth even among incoming freshmen at Wheaton College, one of our finest Christian schools. Published on August 9, 1999, it read, "We live in a postbiblical era where general knowledge of the Bible cannot be assumed. We may lament the neglect of the Bible in popular culture and secular education, but we can understand it. But what about the church?"

Perhaps indicating that a little knowledge is a dangerous thing in spiritual as well as financial matters, there is a growing body of evidence that shallow "extrinsic" forms of faith may be more harmful on a purely sociological level than no religion at all. Those same studies still indicate an "intrinsic" faith, where the Spirit has deeply transformed heart, soul, and mind rather than merely finding expression through bumper stickers and bracelets, is the most socially beneficial of all.

We are therefore hearing the same call for an intrinsic and holistic faith from some in the West as we heard from Gandhi. In his book *The Spirit of Democratic Capitalism*, Michael Novak, the recipient of the 1994 Templeton Prize for Progress in Religion, writes,

> There exists no serious disciplined body of theological reflection on the history and foundations of economics. In few areas has Christian theology, in particular, been so little advanced. . . . Corporate executives and workers, white-collar workers and teachers, doctors and lawyers—all have need of spiritual guidance. How can this be given until we have a theology as realistic as the work they do?

Richard John Neuhaus adds, "It is spiritually eviscerating that what millions of men and women do fifty or seventy hours of most every week is bracketed off from their understanding of their faith."

According to Rabbi Dr. Meir Tamari, in the nineteenth-century religious leadership in all religions—Judaism, Christianity, and Islam—"simply abandoned the field of economic morality to the secular world. Religion thus became irrelevant to many people." Adds Tamari in *Religion and Liberty* from the Acton Institute: "We helped to create a split personality among the business leaders. They could be pious men, they could go to church or to synagogue or to the mosque, but religion made no demands on them in the marketplace."

Some contend that the problem is less severe in the Islamic world than in the nominally Christian culture of the West, as it never experienced the Enlightenment that made humankind autonomous from God from Monday to Saturday. Seyyed Hossein Nasr, professor of Islamic studies at George Washington University and one of Islam's foremost scholars, wrote in his book *The Heart Of Islam: Enduring Values for Humanity*:

> The area or activity known as economics as we understand it today was never isolated by itself in Islamic society. It was always combined with ethics and was seen as an organic part of the life of human beings, all of which should be dominated by ethical principles. That is why the very acceptance of economics as an independent domain, not to speak of as the dominating factor in life according to the prevailing paradigms in the modern world, is devastating to the Islamic view of human life. . . . In contrast to the Christian West, where mercantile activity was looked down upon up until the Renaissance, in the Islamic world from the beginning trade and economic transactions were seen in a positive light from the religious point of view. The Prophet himself had originally been a merchant, as had his wife Khadijah, and throughout Islamic history the merchant class associated with the bazaar has been among the most pious in Islamic urban areas, as have been farmers living in the countryside and villages.

Perhaps affirming that *The Economist* was prophetic to publish a special edition on August 6, 1994 about why Islam and the West might be the next global conflict, the moderate and graceful Nasr nevertheless points out that now, "the Islamic world is forced to be involved in a global economic system based on very different tenets and presumptions."

The growing challenges that "casino capitalism" can pose to the religious spirit and ethic can perhaps best be seen in *Forbes* magazine, often called "The Capitalist Tool." The opening page of *The Forbes Scrapbook of Thoughts on the Business of Life* comments on the ethical challenge:

> The moving motive in establishing *Forbes* Magazine in 1917 was ardent desire to promulgate humaneness in business, then woefully lacking. Too many indi-

vidual and corporate employers were merely mercenarily-minded, obsessed only with determination to roll up profits regardless of the suicidal consequences of their shortsighted conduct. They were without consciousness of their civic, social and patriotic responsibilities.

In 1917, the founder of *Forbes* also commented on the spiritual challenge:

> Business was originated to produce happiness, not to pile up millions. Are we in danger of forgetting this? What profiteth it a man to gain uncounted riches if he thereby sacrifices his better self, his nobler qualities of manhood? Mere getting is not living. The man who depends upon his bank account to insure him a happy life reaps disappointment. To the businessman, success heretofore too often has been merely to become rich. That is not a high standard. It is a standard, happily, that is passing.

Mr. Forbes might be disappointed that nearly a century later the magazine he created is not known for honoring the four hundred most ethical and happy people in business but the four hundred richest. The cover of its last edition ranking the world's billionaires even featured "Sex, Money, and Videotape" and honored the king of "trash TV" (March 17, 2003).

When our church and business leaders drift so very far from our spiritual roots, it is virtually inevitable that we will see stories such as the one that appeared in June 2002 in *The Wall Street Journal*. It quoted the highly respected former SEC chairman Arthur Levitt as saying, "Enron is not an aberration. What troubles me is that what is fueling these corporate implosions are not strategic misjudgments, the rise of new competitors, the sudden appearance of rival technologies or even basic managerial mistakes. Instead, it's the uncovering of accounting irregularities, inflated balance sheets and outright corporate deceit and malfeasance." While we should remember that corporate America still has its share of decent leaders, a headline in The Capitalist Tool itself made this confession as 2002 was coming to a close: "We're still a long way from getting straight talk from companies on their profits. The gaps between companies' net income and their own version of earnings are worse than you thought."

This book hopes to narrow that gap by reintegrating faith and finances on the more institutional level as well, such as mutual funds, banks, and so on.

Dr. Drucker's *Post-Capitalist Society* insists that's where our social responsibilities will primarily be met or evaded during coming decades, perhaps centuries. My counseling experience causes me to agree. Our financial world is simply too complex for the typical investor to master. My goal is to help you find those professionals who might manage it at your request. This is compatible with the biblical ethic as Christ established the institution of the church to mediate between the individual and society, much as our mutual funds and banks do. We will therefore explore primarily how the biblical spirit and ethic might inform both attitudes and behavior of Christians who choose which institutions to entrust with the management of God's resources.

Prior to that, however, it is important to understand and evaluate widely accepted attitudes and principles that may be preventing us from trusting *any* institution to manage our money. Primary among them are accepting nonbiblical principles as though they were gospel simply because they come from Christian ministries. That is the purpose of the first two chapters. From there we will move on to principles and ideas that I hope will spark in readers a vision for a more spiritual and ethical world, overflowing with true abundance and committed to sharing this abundance with all of creation.

Part I

The Desert Detour around True Riches

∽

"We do not have a theology of public life yet. So in the political sphere, we went from unthinking noninvolvement to unthinking involvement. We do have public spokespersons like Jerry Falwell and Pat Robertson, but they really haven't thought these issues through theologically. The result is that the theological basis for what their political followers have advocated has been at best minimal and at worst perverse."

Rev. Dr. Richard Mouw, President, Fuller Theological Seminary

CHAPTER ONE

MONEY AS RELIGION

"The other day I met with a Chinese dissident who has served time in jail, and whose husband is in jail in Beijing. I asked her if the longing for democratic principles that has swept the generation of Tiananmen Square has been accompanied by a rise in religious feeling—a new interest in Buddhism, Taoism, Christianity. She thought for a moment and looked at me. 'Among the young, I would say our religion is money,' she said. I nodded and said, 'Oh, that's our religion too.'"

Peggy Noonan, editorial board member of the *Wall Street Journal*

IT HAS BEEN RIGHTLY NOTED that the leaders of some of America's worst turn-of-the-millennium corporate scandals were devoted churchgoers — even Sunday school teachers and ministry board members—who fell prey to the lure of wanting far more than what they already had and needed. That has happened throughout history. What seems new to some is that it has become the norm rather than an aberration. Author Jacob Needleman writes in *Money and the Meaning of Life*, "Money in the modern era is a purely secular force. . . . Cut off from any relation to spiritual aspiration, it has become the most obvious example of a fire raging out of control." As the above quote from Peggy Noonan, former President Reagan's favorite speechwriter attests, it is rapidly becoming a global fire.

Some biblical teachings are easy to state and easy to understand, but very hard to follow because they are contrary to *base* human nature. Foremost among such teachings is Jesus' warning that it is impossible to serve the "two masters" of God and mammon, meaning money that demands humanity's service rather than money that serves humanity's demands. Unfortunately, human nature yearns for money, or more accurately, for the security and prestige of what it will buy. If Americans *really* loved money, our national savings rate wouldn't be even lower than our national giving rate!

While disturbing, any effort to set forth a biblical guide to faithful finances must include a strong affirmation of this truth. The love of material things is epidemic in our society, and the Christian community is not exempt. Peter Wehner, director of public policy at the conservative political think tank Empower America, has written:

> The New Testament says much more about the dangers riches pose to one's soul than it does about many well-publicized issues about which many Christians feel so strongly. Yet you would never know this by the agenda advanced by America's most prominent and politically active Christian organizations, magazines, and radio talk shows. . . . In pursuit of wealth and worldly pleasures, Christians have become virtually indistinguishable from the rest of the world. We have bought into non-Christian precepts. Note the irony: Christians seeking and encouraging others to seek that which our Lord repeatedly warned against.

The Prosperity Gospel and Jabez's Prayer

The virtual worship of money throughout much of the Christian world is not only tolerated in both subtle and not-so-subtle ways, but in some segments of our community, material wealth is irrevocably linked with mature and growing faith. Such is the case with proponents of the so-called prosperity gospel, which essentially promises that those who are faithful have no choice but to be rich as well. To be otherwise is a sign of spiritual weakness.

This teaching remains alive and well, even though some of its former advocates, including Jim Bakker, who rose to prominence in the 1980s with the PTL television ministry, regret ever being associated with it. After Bakker spent some time in prison actually studying the Bible, he wrote in *Prosperity and the Coming Apocalypse* that he had been an "unwitting false prophet," presenting "a Disneyland gospel, in which the good guys always get rich." He added: "I, like so many of my former colleagues, had merely been preaching what I had heard some other preachers say. I passed along things I had read in somebody else's books, rather than carefully examining Scriptures to see what God had to say."

In his book *Toxic Faith,* author Stephen Arterburn identifies prosperity gospel teaching as a source of toxic faith. He writes, "If, in your toxic faith, you believe that the more faithful you are, the more material gain you will get, you can look forward to great disappointment.... Although wealth is not bad, and can be a great blessing, it is no indicator of spiritual strength."

Because toxic faith is still alive and well in American Christianity, it should come as no surprise that the book *The Prayer of Jabez*, by Bruce Wilkinson, took the country by storm. This prayer, found in 1 Chronicles 4:10, reads, "And Jabez called on the God of Israel saying, 'Oh, that you would bless me indeed, and enlarge my territory, that Your hand would be with me, and that You would keep me from evil, that I may not cause pain!' So God granted him what he requested" (New King James Version).

Many of my closest friends love this book. Without exception, they repeat the author's contention that "enlarge my territory" is about increasing influence for ministry, not material gain. But page 31 indicates otherwise, for Wilkinson writes; "If Jabez had worked on Wall Street, he might have prayed, 'Lord, increase the value of my investment portfolios.' When I talk to presidents of companies, I often talk to them about this particular mind-set. When Christian executives ask me, 'Is it right for me to ask God for more business?' my response is, 'Absolutely!'"

That is why I believe this prayer is dangerous when isolated from the larger, paradoxical ethic of wealth creation found in the Bible. One must consider, for example, that the Jabez prayer appears to negate the blessing of Abraham, who preferred brotherhood to prime grazing lands (Genesis 13:8–9) and the famous prayer of Solomon, who was blessed by God with riches simply because he had *the faith to pray for wisdom rather than riches* (1 Kings 3:7–13). But Jabez seems to assure that we can care little about brotherhood when investing and know little or nothing about the economy, stock valuations, or the Y2K computer problem, yet God will still entrust us with significant wealth. On page 84, Wilkinson writes: "I promise that you will see a direct link: You will know beyond doubt that God has opened heaven's storehouses *because you prayed* (emphasis his)." Particularly in a bear market, that is a promise likely to be broken, and likely to cause people to doubt the power of true prayer.

It should be no small concern that millions of Christians may now be praying the obscure prayer of Jabez each day, as the author recommends, rather than reciting the Lord's Prayer. Jabez asked God to "enlarge my territory," which is a nice *want* or even *desire*. Jesus, in contrast, taught us to ask simply for "daily bread," which we all *need*. And then he asked that God's gracious will be done in matters of wants and desires. Down through history, moral philosophers such as Tolstoy have reminded us that all the territory a person really needs is a six-foot plot for burial, which our Lord actually had to borrow temporarily as he had lost his influence over even Peter.

The likely reason for the overwhelming popularity of *The Prayer of Jabez* is that it essentially syncretizes Christianity with the selfish individualism and materialism of our age. Jabez teaches us to pray in a self-centered way that God will "bless *me* . . . enlarge *my* territory. . . be with *me* and keep *me* from evil." Christ taught us a humbler prayer focused on God and neighbor: "*our* Father . . . *thy* name . . . *thy* kingdom" (rather than *my* territory).

In his book *A Culture of Prosperity,* Rev. James Mulholland writes: "In significant ways *The Prayer of Jabez* is counter to the heart of the gospel and the priorities of Jesus. It represents the advancement of self and the resistance to self-denial Jesus confronted in his day and God continues to challenge within Christianity. And, although Mr. Wilkinson has tried to redeem the words of Jabez, he has only succeeded in fanning into flame the embers of a prosperity theology many had hoped was finally dying."

The first businessman who ever quoted the prayer of Jabez to me led a Christian business whose parent company was on the verge of bankruptcy. This devout friend managed his division quite astutely. Yet despite mentioning the prayer nearly each time we talked, his stock in the parent company, which was once worth millions, did nothing but decline to the point of being worthless. He lived with great stress for more than a year as he contemplated the fates of dozens of Christian employees, shareholders, and clients. At a time when most men retire, he was forced from the company he founded and isn't sure how he can survive in the future.

Beyond disappointing an untold number of its followers, *The Prayer of Jabez* has afforded the secular press another opportunity to give the Christian faith a black eye. A *New York Times* review on May 8, 2001 quoted Dr. Jeffrey Mahan, professor of ministry, media and culture at Iliff School of Theology in Denver, as saying the book "fits with the narcissism of the age. Religious life is focused on me and my needs."

The New Republic's June 6, 2001 review of Wilkinson's book, headlined "Christianity Gets Easy: Indulgences," stated:

Critics dismiss *The Prayer of Jabez* as just another self-help book, a kind of *Seven Habits of Highly Blessed People* that reduces religion's great insights to six easy-to-follow steps. But it's actually more feeble than that. The real genius of Jabez is that, in many ways, it is the ultimate anti-self-help book. . . . Wilkinson gives us a blueprint for being good—even godly—even as he relieves us from the risk, pressure and guilt that go with personal responsibility. Then he guarantees immediate results. Thus, it may be that the Jabez craze is driven not so much by our insatiable desire to be richer, thinner, more significant—but by our exhaustion in the effort. It's why liposuction replaced aerobics and why we all bought into the idea that the cyberboom would make us rich without our really trying.

Both *The Wall Street Journal* and *Newsweek* called the book "New Age," meaning it, too, had essentially turned God's spiritual kingdom into Disney's Magic Kingdom. The *London Times* said it showed how spiritually "gullible" Americans are to think that all they have to do to grow rich is to pray a scripted prayer. Personally, I saw the book as a clear cultural indicator that the fear of the 1990s had finally given way to greed, even euphoria, and sold most of my stocks as the new millennium began. You will better understand how that is a part of the biblical ethic as we progress.

Daniel L. Gard, dean of the graduate school at Concordia Theological Seminary, wrote at www.issuesetc.org:

American culture is very oriented toward paychecks and big houses. This basically gives those same secular values a religious shellacking. So you can feel good as a religious person and at the same time go after all the stuff in the world. It attempts to give a Christianizing to some of the worst characteristics of our culture. You throw in a little God talk, and now it becomes an immediately sellable thing.

Putting Money in Its Proper Place

There is much practical wisdom in the biblical admonitions to put money in its proper place. In fact, the religion of money has been accompanied by an epidemic of anxiety and depression in our increasingly prosperous culture, an epidemic that touched this aging baby boomer until I started down a new path of remembering and discovering those things that truly provide meaning in life.

Near the beginning of our new millennium, an article in *Forbes* magazine posed the question: "Feeling down, anxious?" It continued, "Your problem may be that fat bank account. New research says the hell-bent pursuit of money can be hazardous to your mental health. . . . It turns out that having money is fine—lusting after it as a paramount motivation is the problem. There's no drawback to having money. You just need to remember the things that truly provide meaning in life."

An article that appeared in Reuters News Service in July 2001 reported that Australian researchers found

> positive correlation between materialism—or an "excessive concern" for material things—and negative psychological phenomena, such as depression, anxiety, and anger. Said Shaun Saunders, one of the authors of the report from the University of Newcastle, Australia, "If your self-worth is invested in what you own, as can be the case in our market-driven society, then these things may not hold their value for very long." Ironically, many resort to shopping sprees to lift their gloom. Says Saunders, "This may give a person a sense of control through owning something, but the research shows that materialism is negatively correlated with life satisfaction."

Both *The Wall Street Journal* and *The Economist* magazine have detailed the magnitude of the epidemic of anxiety and depression. Spirituality and healthcare costs aside, people suffering from such depression are not as productive. This is economically significant as America approaches a time when fewer and fewer workers will support more and more retirees. Each worker will need to be most productive if America is to maintain its standard of living—which is not my primary concern about the future but a concern of many nonetheless.

Materialism's grip on the Christian culture is evidenced in part by the way we treat people who have a lot of money. For example, Henri Nouwen often cautioned us about churches, colleges, and ministries that too often treat major donors as "religious royalty," making it necessary for us to "retreat to silence in order to hear the more humbling voice of God." We need to be mindful that if success were defined by the accumulation, inheritance, and giving of money, then Moses, Jesus, and Paul must be counted among those who failed. Perhaps that is why Mother Teresa liked to say that God does not call us to success, but to faithfulness. Perhaps that is why she considered wealth, not poverty, to be the single greatest threat to her ministry. Jesus asked, "What does it prosper a man to gain the whole world but lose his soul?" But this spiritual question does not sell as well as the fear-filled "Whatever happened to the American Dream?"

The times call not just for tweaking Christian people's understanding of what it means to be faithful in our finances, but for a wholesale shift. This shift begins with the recognition that all we have ultimately belongs to God. It ends by acknowledging the tension between The Kingdom of God and The American Dream. To put it another way, in order to be faithful in our finances, we must resolve consciously to use *all* of God's wealth—100 percent of the time, talent, and treasure with which we have been entrusted—for the glory of God as well as for the benefit of others and ourselves.

This shift means having faith that if we're doing what we are supposed to be doing today, God will take care of the future and we won't waste our prayers reminding God that every human being wants more and more. That means we must often tune out those with their own designs for that future.

ᔥ CHAPTER TWO ᔆ

TUNING OUT FALSE PROPHETS

"The true prophet does not engage in political diatribe to provide a rally-
ing point for any particular course or action. He questions all the pow-
ers that be in the name of the one Power beyond them."

James Sanders, author of *Torah and Canon*

IN THE EARLY 1990S, one of my wife's best friends, a beautiful young
mother of two, told my wife over coffee one morning that even though she
was living the American Dream she was deeply worried about her economic
future. When she had finished describing her worst imaginings, I asked why
she was so pessimistic about the future. She responded that a prominent
conservative televangelist had been sharing a most negative economic vision.
A best-selling evangelical author and radio commentator had been saying the
same. Thus, she concluded, the bad news had to be true.

Our friend was a Roman Catholic. But she had never heard that since the
collapse of the Berlin Wall in 1989, Pope John Paul II had been sharing the
good news about a "new springtime of the human spirit," which should have
had positive ramifications for the future of the economy. While he had not
bothered predicting that economy specifically, he had been quite active in
suggesting that capitalism needed to be circumscribed in a moral framework. She had not heard that good news either.

That was the first of many times during the '90s and on into the twenty-
first century that I would notice that the economic worldviews of many
Catholics, mainline Christians, Baptists, and evangelicals were not being
shaped by the biblical ethic or by the leaders of their own denominations.
Those worldviews were also rarely shaped by the sophisticated financial
media, such as *The Economist* or *The Wall Street Journal*. Rather, the popular but simplistic thinking of the secular and evangelical media shaped them.

Interestingly, a politician, child psychologist, engineer, accountant, and an occasional pastor typically dominated the evangelical media shaping those economic worldviews. If any had true economic or investment training and insight, it typically wasn't very evident during the greatest economic expansion and bull market in history.

Despite their oft-stated contempt for each other over political and cultural matters, through the past two decades, the Christian and secular media alike regularly advanced a common message of doom and gloom. Even *The New York Times* repeatedly ran a full-page ad for a time featuring a frail and frightened man sitting atop a splitting earth. The caption beneath was devastatingly simple: "These Times Demand *The Times.*" Such a message, implying that the world was falling apart, typifies what American Christians were also being fed by several prominent evangelical authors, speakers, and ministries.

Actually, the degree of gloom and doom emanating from the religious media was much more serious. After all, while the secular media considered Desert Storm to be little more than a brief skirmish with a second-rate power, the evangelical media told us that Armageddon had arrived. Later in the decade, many of these same icons of the evangelical subculture cited the federal debt and the horrors that would result from Y2K as focal points of a dismal future in these supposed last days. And we were told repeatedly that our $5 trillion federal debt had destroyed our children's futures. The implication always seemed to be that the debt was clear evidence that our government was evil, when it may have been acting most biblically.

In short, for much of the past two decades, the evangelical economic worldview has been shaped by such fear-filled questions as, "Why invest when the world is ending?" "Whatever happened to the American Dream?" "What if the federal debt bankrupts America?" "What if Y2K results in economic chaos?" and "Won't investing with an ethical and prudent spirit produce a less abundant life?"

In his faith-filled Sermon on the Mount, Jesus answered those fear-filled questions by telling his followers that only pagans worry about the economic future (Matthew 5–6). But this did not stop evangelical leaders from advising us to hoard United States Treasury bills (t-bills) and gold coins, since the sky was falling. Investors who followed this advice in the '90s today know better than anyone how deeply they were led astray. One, a client who is an elderly single woman who attended a terror-filled "Christian financial conference" nearly ten years ago, is still hoarding t-bills today.

Henri Nouwen, who taught at Harvard, Yale, and Notre Dame, has written:

> The agenda of the world—the issues and items that fill our newspapers and newscasts—is an agenda of fear and power. A huge network of anxious questions surrounds us and begins to guide many, if not most of our daily decisions. Clearly, those who can pose these fearful questions which bind us have true power over us. [But] fearful questions never lead to love-filled answers. . . . A careful look at the gospels show that Jesus seldom accepted the questions posed to him. He exposed them as coming from the house of fear. They did not belong to the house of God.

In Jeremiah 23:30–32, God told the prophet and people of Israel, as well as us: "Therefore I am against the prophets who steal from one another words supposedly from me. They lead my people astray with their reckless lies, yet I did not send them. They do not benefit these people in the least." While the April 22, 2002 issue of *Christianity Today* observed that "businesses marketing books to conservative Christians go to great pains to avoid offending them," true prophets from Moses to Jeremiah to Paul have always spoken the difficult truth that the human condition is not always pretty. As uncomfortable as their words may make us, they have also always spoken the *very* difficult truth that the condition of God's leaders, and therefore God's people, is often no prettier. And the Scriptures tell us that judgment begins in the house of the Lord. So I would guess that if Jesus were to return today, one question he might ask is: "If religious media leaders are preoccupied with making wildly erroneous predictions about the future rather than teaching sound financial ethics for today and believe America's problems are 'the economy stupid,' can we really expect better of Wall Street analysts, corporate CEOs and politicians?"

I take no joy in criticizing fellow believers. But, in a book on faithful finances I would be remiss not to call attention to widely accepted economic teachings whose scriptural basis is at the least questionable, if not totally misguided. I am confident I am not alone in my perspectives. Several prominent evangelical leaders have repeatedly expressed to me their disapproval of the sensationalist doom-and-gloom views that have found an all-too-ready marketplace, though they are hesitant to disagree publicly with a fellow evangelical leader. As this book will explore, however, and as too many Catholic bishops have recently been reminded, the biblical ethic does not advocate silence as a strategy for the abundant life. As has been well said, all it takes for evil to prevail is for good people to do nothing.

Jeremiah, therefore, seems particularly relevant in our age of mass-marketed media messages, comical corporate balance sheets, and painted political platforms. For other than Jesus, of all the characters in the Bible, Jeremiah was uniquely capable of humbly seeing and proclaiming difficult realities of the present while remaining unshakably hopeful of the economic future—as evidenced by his buying of a field during desperate times (Jeremiah 32:15). No see-no-evil optimism. No sky-is-falling pessimism. No acting like a politician rather than a statesman in order to win votes. No fudging of corporate balance sheets to tempt Wall Street investors. No turning God's Word upside-down in order to attract followers, increase territory or influence, or raise funds. And, no beating around the bush to avoid offending self-anointed prophets who seem to be day trading our souls.

America's True Deficit: Spiritual Leadership

"All of the great leaders have had one characteristic in common: it was to confront unequivocally the major anxiety of their people in their time. This, and not much else, is the essence of leadership."

Professor John Kenneth Galbraith

Historically, Christian leaders have tended to assure destitute people of God's provision and remind those with excess that it endangers their souls. But in 1992, as the richest country in the history of the world was recovering from the lightest recession of the post-war period, the Christian Booksellers Association named as its "Book of the Year" a book lamenting that America's economy would no longer produce enough goods and services, primarily because of the federal debt. It was titled *The Coming Economic Earthquake* and was written by Larry Burkett. A household name among conservative evangelicals, Burkett offers financial advice directly through some one thousand evangelical radio stations and indirectly through many evangelical ministries around the country.

Burkett's advice places a premium on minimizing or eliminating debt. To his possible credit, during the 1980s and '90s he encouraged tens of thousands of debt-burdened Christians to give up their credit cards, reduce their mortgages, and become more generous givers to evangelical ministries. I say "possible" as their actions were typically motivated by fear, which is spiritually impoverishing. And his earthquake prediction was unfortunately not the first time this Christian leader had forecast a dismal future. In fact, the book simply reset the doomsday clock that many evangelicals seem never to tire of watching. In the book's foreword, Burkett wrote that even during the early 1980s he had "felt compelled by the Lord" to share his belief that no economy could absorb forever the amount of debt the U.S. economy was accumulating. At that time, he had predicted the economy would collapse within ten years. When that didn't happen, rather than reconsider his economic worldview, he wrote his bestseller that postponed judgment day.

Another decade later, Burkett began the new millennium by writing a study guide for the Southern Baptists entitled *Jesus on Money*. In it, Burkett was still declaring, "Scripture clearly indicates that borrowing is not normal to God's plan and was never intended to be used as a routine part of our financial planning." But in his Sermon on the Mount, Jesus actually said, "when someone wants to borrow something, lend it to him" (Matthew 5:42) and "if you lend only to those from whom you hope to get it back, why should you receive a blessing?" (Luke 6:34). Moses actually taught that it is "evil" *not* to lend (Deuteronomy 15:9), which obviously means some Israelites had to borrow. Moses, therefore, developed laws that all those loans should be forgiven each seventh and fiftieth year.

The important point is that Burkett's cultural reading of the Scriptures caused millions of supposedly Bible-believing Christians to adopt an extremely negative economic worldview, which had extremely negative consequences for their spirits and finances, particularly if they were investors rather than credit-card borrowers. That, in turn, caused most to adopt a decidedly negative attitude towards the government that the apostle Paul asked us to "honor and obey" (Romans 13).

Ironically, some of us more moderate Republicans believe Burkett's advice had negative political consequences. The second edition of his *Earthquake* book was published in 1994 and Burkett wrote in the introduction: "These books [concerning the federal debt] along with Ross Perot, helped to focus the election of 1992 around the economy and because of it, President Bush lost his job" to Governor Clinton, who exploited the economic misperceptions with the campaign theme, "It's the economy, stupid."

A lot of congressional representatives lost their jobs in 1994 during Newt Gingrich's angry revolution. That, too, may have been largely because of Burkett, who wrote in the same influential introduction:

> I have had the opportunity to address members of the Congress several times, as well as sit in on many policy-making discussions about our economy. I am continually amazed at how so many intelligent people can be so confused over such a simple issue of debt. Most average income Americans understand the bottom line very well: You can't spend more than you make forever. . . . It's like a family, in debt up to their ears, who makes just enough to keep their payments current. They can get by unless something unscheduled happens— like a baby, a car breaking down, an accident, or an illness. They start down the road to disaster. This country is so far down the road to disaster now that, in my opinion, there is very little that can be done to avert it.

But as we will see, true economists never saw the federal debt, either morally or economically, as being as negative and extreme as Burkett encouraged his listeners and readers to see it.

While I have myself now achieved a debt-free lifestyle, I've also grown to believe that Burkett causes people to view personal and corporate debt too negatively. For example, he often quotes a verse about the borrower being the servant, or slave, of the lender, without explaining the cultural context of the ancient passage. As Professor Justo Gonzalez wrote in his marvelous book *Faith and Wealth*: "Contrary to our common assumptions, slaves in the Roman Empire were not always poor nor always powerless. As economic historian M. I. Finley has stated, slaves 'did the same kind of civilian work as their free counterparts, in the same ways and under the same conditions.'"

In other words, while we must make use of debt prudently, the Bible takes a far more balanced view of the subject than many of us have been led to embrace. Still, it is not at all unusual for an evangelical client to say it is wrong to use modest debt to build a church. Some of these clients are an unfortunate example of how that perspective can divest the kingdom because they are unwittingly invested in junk bond mutual funds that finance almost the entire cost of constructing casinos.

Larry Burkett has been far from alone in making extreme economic forecasts that cause us to invest contrary to the biblical ethic. In early 1984, a potential client showed me a personal letter he had received from media celebrity Pat Robertson. He had written Robertson because he had sold his stocks on Robertson's advice and they had moved higher. Robertson's response assured him: "It is my feeling now, as it was last year, that the economy of the United States and the world is in an extremely precarious position. The banking system is overloaded with hundreds of billions of bad loans and any day there is a very real danger of a major default which could conceivably trigger a banking collapse. This will mean, when it comes, that the stock market is going to go down and that only the most liquid securities such as United States Treasury bills will prove to be good investments."

The stock market would triple during the 1980s despite Robertson's take on things. But in 1990, Robertson wrote his influential book entitled *The New Millennium*. A chapter called "The New Economics" confidently predicted: "At some point government debt may become worthless; and we are faced with the very real prospect of a stock market collapse coupled with a collapse of the dollar and the government bond market. The prospect is for depression followed by runaway inflation." Robertson's confused economics were then matched by this confusing advice for our personal finances: "People would be well advised to avoid the stock market until the smoke clears to have available investments of the safest and most liquid sort, such as U.S. Treasury bills. The government will never default. . . . " (As a tip to novice investors, if you ever feel our government's debt is becoming worthless, there may be better options for your life-savings than that same government's treasury bills as treasury bills are part of the federal debt!)

Robertson's extreme worldview and sensational prophecies caused the stock of his broadcasting company to soar and his political influence to grow. But, they also kept fearful viewers buying the treasury bills that financed the deficits of a supposedly bankrupt government. The damage to spirits, and particularly to minds, was surely much greater than the damage done directly to portfolios.

Grant Jeffrey's 1995 book *Final Warning: Economic Collapse and the Coming World Government* was marketed widely in the evangelical media—as have been several more recent "final" warnings. Jeffrey's book featured the endorsements of several well-known evangelical media celebrities. One of the book's chapters, titled "The Coming Economic Collapse," demonstrated little of the humility evident among most seasoned economists and investment advisors when predicting the future, much less the humility of Moses and Jesus.

At a time when the U.S. stock market was around the 5000 level and ready to more than double, Jeffrey's chapter titled "The Coming Stock Market Crash" began: "We are facing the greatest risk of a stock market crash since 1929." The author continued, "At the same time, millions of naive, inexperienced investors are pouring their life-savings into a staggering array of mutual funds. . . . The situation is far more dangerous today than it was in 1929. . . ." A section titled "The Banking-Credit Crisis" even prophesied, "The present insolvency of the FDIC makes it *a certainty* that millions will lose their life-savings in a future banking collapse" (emphasis mine). Ironically, in the book's closing chapter, "Financial Strategies for the Last Days," the author writes: "One of the safest and easiest investment choices for the very conservative investor is an investment in government savings bonds offered by both the U.S. and Canadian governments." Apparently, the author had not lost all faith in the good old bankrupt U.S. government to magically compound our money in the few days we have left!

The list of deplorable economic predictions and short-sighted financial advice from evangelical leaders goes on. Despite my own efforts to discourage it, television preacher D. James Kennedy produced an hour-long television special about the supposed horrors of the federal debt. And in the opening pages of his influential book *Storm Shelter,* Ron Blue wrote, "The family has mortgaged its future. The federal government, by continuing to spend more than its income, has done the same. . . . As the deficit mushrooms, the future becomes less and less secure. . . . Many of our dreams—in fact, the American dream itself—seem to be vanishing into an early-morning fog."

It should be said again that these worldviews are not biblical since the Bible assures us that earthquakes, storms, and fog are quite normal and will not halt God's gracious provision. That is why Jesus asked Peter to step out of the boat and into the storm rather than sheltering him from it. Nor were those worldviews economic, as we will see. They were political, with most being focused on the supposed financial sins of our government. Robertson began his chapter on "The New Economics" by saying, "The specter of massive debt overhangs the world economy. American debt ratios are dramatically more threatening in 1990 than in 1929. Going into the 1990s, the United States Government has direct debt of three trillion dollars and contingent liabilities of some six and one-half trillion dollars." Robertson failed to mention the hope-filled fact that our federal debt to GNP ratio was actually only one-half of what it was at the end of World War II. Including that information might have turned political anger to spiritual hope.

Fortunately for our family's finances, at the end of World War II, my father didn't have much time to listen to media pundits selling books on the subject of the federal debt. He and millions like him returned home from the war and went to work to grow the ecomoy, effectively paying the debt down. And he prospered throughout the blissful 1950s, as did our nation.

During the early 1990s, some of my conservative clients listened and read as our politicians, media, and ministries demonized the size of the debt without discussing the size of our assets. By focusing on the negative, most who listened missed the opportunity to prosper from the greatest bull market in history. For the record we did have a very, very small handful of more spiritually enlightened evangelical leaders who tried to remind us that from God's perspective, federal debts—indeed whole nations—come and go, but precious and eternal souls should never be destroyed by worry and anxiety.

While the views of Robertson, et al., reflect a very simplistic understanding of the dangers of debt, *The Economist* had this different take on the question: "In 'Hamlet,' Polonius famously advised his son Laertes 'neither a borrower nor lender be.' But that was bad economics: a certain amount of debt is healthy, even desirable. Poor countries often have low domestic debt levels; as they develop, debt will tend to rise. It is better that surplus savings be lent than lie under mattresses." It is disheartening that many Christians believe "neither a borrower nor lender be" is a biblical concept rather than an Elizabethan axiom. Debt can be a sign of trust and productivity.

Economist Francis Cavanaugh, the senior career executive responsible for debt management policy advice in the Treasury Department, received the Presidential Rank Award of Distinguished Executive from Presidents Jimmy Carter, Ronald Reagan, and George Bush. In his book *The Truth about the Federal Debt*, Cavanaugh explained how marketing and the pursuit of votes rather than leadership and the pursuit of truth played key roles in the confusion about the federal debt: "Most of the confusion over the burden of the debt arises from the understandable tendency to try to model government financing after the financing of an individual family or business. Politicians often add to this confusion." He then basically explained that families and businesses are not sovereign nations with the authority to levy taxes, print currency, and most importantly, to borrow money *from their own citizens,* as well as from other nations, by issuing treasury securities.

In 1992, the same year Burkett's book was published, the biblically literate, politically conservative, and economically educated editor of *The Wall Street Journal,* Robert Bartley, published his little-read book called *The Seven Fat Years.* Wrote Bartley, "The deficit is not a meaningless figure, only a grossly overrated one. . . . Our politicians have conjured the deficit into a bogeyman with which to scare themselves . . . but behind this political symbol, we need to understand the economic reality, or lack of it. . . . [I]n the advanced economic literature, the big debate is over whether deficits matter *at all*" (emphasis his). That was because, contrary to popular belief, about 90 percent of the federal debt had been borrowed from Americans, not from foreigners. And it was foreign debt that was the true concern in even Old Testament days—before Jesus turned foreigners into neighbors, as we will see.

As Bartley, Sir John Templeton, and other leading economists such as President Reagan's budget director David Stockman predicted at the beginning of the 1990s, our federal debt ratios would plunge during the decade as our economy grew, just as it did after World War II. Indeed, as the new millennium began, Bartley wrote, "As for the debt, it's plunging. The OMB predicts that by 2011 it will be 6.1% of GDP, the lowest level since 1917. Government debt can be worrisome at a high enough rate—more than 100% of economic output at the end of World War II or in Japan today. But at current levels it's a mere curiosity. Letting it displace growth as the centerpiece of economic policy is eccentric and potentially destructive." And certainly, allowing it to displace the biblical spirit and ethic is even more eccentric and destructive.

As I said, the evangelical subculture has not been without voices of moderation. Unfortunately, Christian books are typically sold by authors who appear in the Christian media, and that media rarely invites authors who question what the media has been telling people. So few evangelicals have read the book *Safe and Sound: Why You Can Stand Secure on the Future of the U.S. Economy* by Bruce Howard, professor of economics at Wheaton College, a mecca of thoughtful evangelicalism. Howard, concerned about the economic confusion that politically oriented religious broadcasters had created, wrote:

> Credit certainly is a pervasive element of the modern market economy. And if there is one element in the market economy that has caused more confusion in the minds of Christians than anything else, it is the issue of credit. . . . We have to see a distinction can be made between *production loans* and *consumption loans.* . . . As with individuals, debt for governments is neither inherently bad nor good. . . . Government debt is justified when the proceeds of the debt are used to finance something that provides both current and future benefits to taxpayers.

This perspective has solid grounding in both the Bible and Judeo-Christian tradition. The great Jewish philosopher Maimonides even *favored* productive lending, and therefore borrowing, over charity, because the lending enabled the job creation that made charity unnecessary. The Protestant Reformers later encouraged those with capital but no productive ideas to lend it to those with productive ideas but no capital, which is a pretty good definition of capitalism as it should be.

We need to understand the nuance that modest amounts of debt used for productive purposes, such as winning the Cold War as our government did or by producing goods and services as corporate America has done, is morally legitimate, even recommended by the biblical ethic. That was a key insight of the Protestant Reformers that made banking, capitalism, and even modernity possible. One could make a case that our material wealth in the West is a direct result of Luther and Calvin having a deeper understanding of the Bible's teachings about the productive uses of debt than many of our political-religious leaders do today.

In short, true economists know that a healthy level of debt can be a tool for the creation of jobs, housing, companies, airports, roads, and other infrastructures. As with alcoholic beverages, if we have the discipline to handle credit, we ought to use it in a responsible way. Those who do not have such discipline would be better off avoiding it. But all of us need to reject efforts to rewrite what Moses and Jesus taught the world in order to suit the purposes of our religious subculture. There are some American ministries trying to help millions of desperately poor people in the Third World who need tiny productive loans in order to create jobs and feed their families. They should not be denied by our self-serving theologies claiming that borrowing and lending are unbiblical.

From Selling Fear to Proclaiming Faith

The most widely promulgated economic advice emanating from influential Christian leaders is rooted in fear-filled bad news rather than love-filled good news. (Thousands of planes arriving safely each day don't make a very sellable headline even if they are reality.) The problem goes far beyond the issue of the national debt. In the late 1990s, Burkett told his fellow religious broadcasters that Y2K could be "the most serious threat to our economy since the Great Depression." That was when I realized what I thought was negative politics was actually negative worldview. I then wrote a cover story for the National Religious Broadcasters' magazine entitled "Y2K: The Bug That Ate Stewardship" and began writing this book.

Focus on the Family broadcasts sold books about a looming catastrophe, as well as tapes about how to survive the impending doom. Both were sadly detailed in a front-page, column-one, *Wall Street Journal* story. Jerry Falwell did the same and received a scolding in an *Economist* article entitled "Doom and Dollars." Justo Gonzalez wrote in *Faith and Wealth* that early Christians who wondered how to determine true prophets from false prophets often consulted the ancient *Didache,* which advised them, "An apostle or prophet who asks for more than bread for the road—especially one who asks for money—or one who asks to be put up for more than two days is false." It might greatly reduce the number of wild predictions and refocus us on financial ethics if more of us meditate on that ancient counsel occasionally.

Perhaps the best example of profiting as a result of a sensationalistic end-times message is the "Left Behind" series, a best-selling line of novels with sales in the millions. Again, while Luther's Small Catechism indicates he would have thought the theology contained in the novels was biblically questionable, someone has placed the entire series in my Lutheran church's library. The series exposes American Christians' strange obsession with the end of the world but doesn't mention that Luther thought an advancing army was a sign that the end was near way back then. Yet when some of us gathered at a friend's house to welcome in 2003, a fellow church member told me that she had read every book in the series.

Our obsession is not without potentially serious consequences for the abundant life, both economically and politically. As I have explained in previous books, few people give or invest for the future when they don't believe there's going to be one. And late in 2002, *The Economist* ran a lengthy editorial entitled, "Behold the Rapture: Millenarianism is becoming a force on the right in American politics." Following is an excerpt:

> To many people, particularly Europeans, the Rapture comes from UFO-watching, conspiracy-obsessed fringes of American life, where "X-Files" enthusiasts meet the Montana Freemen to stockpile supplies in a cave. Apart from marveling at the varieties of religious experience, one's natural reaction to it is a Gallic shrug. Such things hardly merit political attention. Not this year. Millenarianism—the belief in the thousand-year reign of King Jesus—is *starting to spill out over its narrow banks and is flooding towards the mainstream.* Conservative radio stations across the sunbelt have been full of this stuff since September 11th. But the best evidence comes from the phenomenon called the "Left Behind" series—a best-selling sequence of novels, whose sales have soared in the past year, that dramatize American's strange obsession with the end of the world. . . . Amongst the millenarian mayhem, "Left Behind" has a not-very-hidden-agenda. It is no accident, for example, that the poor old UN is Antichrist's chosen vehicle. International agencies and supra-national currencies are works of the devil. . . . As McCarthyism showed, the demons of zealotry, once unleashed, can be devastating (emphasis mine).

But "Left Behind" was not the first of the genre to have arrived on the scene. Hal Lindsey is the author of *The Late Great Planet Earth.* He was cited by *The New York Times* as the best-selling "nonfiction" author in the world during the 1970s. Despite the earth still turning, Lindsey is still out there, giving lectures, selling books, and hosting a television show. He has even recently launched a newspaper, which is somewhat ironic given his contention that we are living in the last days. An elderly widowed client sent me a flyer promoting it that said: "We are living in the last days—the evidence is all around us. The *Last Days Chronicles* is an exciting new newspaper dedicated to examining that evidence—taken directly from the daily news."

Since Lindsey has been at the fringes of American Christianity for decades, I paid little attention to the flyer. I paid far more attention a few days later when my *Christianity Today* shared an interview with Franklin Graham in which he emphasized: "We're living in the last days. Don't hide your head in the sand." *CT* did not bother to remind the passionate but independent thinking younger Graham, or the millions he is suddenly influencing, that C. S. Lewis once wrote in *The World's Last Night and Other Essays:*

> We must never speak to simple, excitable people about "the Day" without emphasizing again and again the utter impossibility of prediction. We must try to show them that that impossibility is an essential part of the doctrine. If you do not believe our Lord's words, why do you believe in his return at all (see Mark 13:32)? And if you do believe them, must you not put away from you, utterly and forever, any hope of dating that return?

Reflecting today's confusion over the Christian worldview and the ironies that confusion produces in our daily world, my next *CT* (December 9, 2002) contained a full-page ad inviting writers to join the Christian Writer's Guild. The ad featured a picture of C. S. Lewis and the headline, "He Made Christianity Irresistible." The Guild is now headed by Jerry Jenkins, the author of the "Left Behind" series, who was pictured along with the sales statistics of the series. In the back of that same issue of *CT*, there was a full-page ad for the *Left Behind* movie and another full-page ad for the new "Left Behind" book. The ad promised, "This spring, no one will escape Armageddon." It should therefore come as no surprise that a company marketing gold coins had bought the back page for an ad with the biblically challenged headline: "Gold: Your Road To Financial Survival." Theologians might wonder what ever happened to manna from God being the Way to the Promised Land.

Indicating that sound theology and economics are not as contradictory as we are often unwittingly taught by Christian publications, the January 4, 2003 edition of *The Economist* observed, without receiving revenues from an ad: "During the past 103 years, American shares have outperformed all other assets, returning 9.3% on average since 1900 compared with 4.8% on long-term Treasury bonds. Gold has yielded a dismal 2.8%, even less than the 4.1% return on cash." My point is that you shouldn't expect even the most reputable evangelical publications to explore why fear is used to sell everything from gold coins to movies and books to the evangelical subculture, even though that fear never seems to enrich those evangelicals doing the buying.

Secular writers don't seem nearly as confused about the effects of fear on the kingdom either. Michael Hill of the *Baltimore Sun* has written:

> Mankind loves an imminent apocalypse. End-of-the-world movements have probably had adherents since the beginning of the world. The top fiction hardcover book on *The New York Times* best-seller list is *The Remnant: Armageddon Is Near*, the latest installment of the immensely popular *Left Behind* series, a dramatization of Christian end-of-the-world prophecies. The problem with such prophecies is that the world, darn it, doesn't end on their schedule. Adherents lose patience and faith.

The way some marketers are leading us away from the Bible and church tradition is objectionable enough. Perhaps even more troubling is the "rarely correct but never in doubt" attitude that accompanies the ideas being advanced. Even after the 1990s progressed pretty much as the economic opposite of what they had predicted, Robertson promoted a 1997 financial conference featuring himself and Burkett with a flyer that described Robertson as "one of America's foremost financial analysts" who would "shed light on what trends to look for in the financial world in the coming months." And a surprising number of people who come to my investment firm still consider the views of Robertson, Burkett, and company not to be the opinions of teflon-coated celebrities but the gospel truth.

Thus the following call for a dose of moderating humility that came from Philip Yancey, writing in *Christianity Today* on July 9, 2001:

> In the 1980s evangelicals on national radio programs fed the AIDS hysteria by warning that HIV could be passed by mosquito bites or contact with toilet seats. In 1999 some evangelical publishers made a fortune on scary predictions about Y2K. Others kept forecasting an economic meltdown during the greatest boom ever. I wonder, is there no place for public apology or at least sheepishness? What would happen if every evangelical institution that profited from scaremongering agreed to place all those profits in a fund to relieve Third World debt? Such notable evangelical "bloopers" demonstrate the point [Wheaton professor] Mark Noll made in his book *The Scandal of the Evangelical Mind*. Few question evangelicalism's passionate heart, and even critics envy its methodology and results, but the evangelical mind may be the movement's weakest link.

As will be more thoroughly developed throughout the rest of this book, economic advice or speculation that is rooted in fear or greed stands in clear violation of the biblical ethic. And its negative effects—spiritual, political, and financial—should neither be underestimated nor taken lightly. Rather we should heed the wisdom of whoever it was who said that worry is like paying interest before it is due on an imaginary loan.

Studies by Independent Sector have consistently cited worry over the economic future *regardless of present realities* as a primary deterrent to charitable giving. Thus, while the fearful worldview sold a few books and tapes for the evangelical media, it has created true spiritual and financial shortages for many of our churches, colleges, ministries, and charities. Indeed, during the decade of the '90s I was told repeatedly by clients that they weren't including the church in their estate plans since their children would need every cent once the Armageddon of Desert Storm, economic earthquake, and Y2K occurred. It was only later in the decade when anxiety turned to confidence and even euphoria that charitable giving surged again and ministries were able to carry out many of the ventures they had only hoped for during previous years. Of course, once the fear over terrorism and/or Islam returned, charitable giving hit another wall.

The truth is that economic negativity has impoverished Christianity and our world in many ways. Fear closes the hand around what one has. While that may be beneficial to those who are spending too much, it is devastating to those who have excess and need to invest or give that excess, rather than hoard it. It is even more devastating to those who need those investments.

Ultimately this book is about the difficult art of creating wealth with these investments without destroying souls in the process. The longer a person studies and practices this art, the more he or she realizes that true prophets may not see the future as much as they see a current reality that most of us will not see for years to come. Part of this reality is that the world our children and grandchildren will live in tomorrow is largely the one we're investing in today.

Yancey also captures this perspective well in another *Christianity Today* column when he wrote:

> The Bible gives us glimpses of the future. Yet it tells us to focus on behavior
> in the present, trusting God with the big picture. Some Christians confuse

those two perspectives. . . . The prophets predicted the Crucifixion, but that does not mean followers of Jesus should have helped nail him to the cross. The New Testament speaks of an Antichrist, but I will not knowingly vote for him even though doing so might hasten the Second Coming. Though I have some hints about the future, I must live in the present, treating the Earth and its people with the same love and care that God invested in them.

Now we must consider why the Antichrist may not need us to "knowingly vote for him" as long as we "unwittingly invest in her." That is, we need to explore why, contrary to the thinking of even our best minds, the biblical ethic still says the "root of all evil" lies in the economic sphere, which has been disproportionately influenced by a female philosopher, rather than in the political sphere.

CHAPTER THREE

ECONOMIES IN CONFLICT,
ETHICS AT WAR

"Love for the poor must be preferential but not exclusive. The leading
sectors of society have been neglected and many people have thus been
estranged from the church. If evangelization of society's leaders is neglected, it should come as no surprise that many who are part of it will be
guided by criteria alien to the Gospel and at times openly hostile to it."

Pope John Paul II

NOW THAT WE HAVE hopefully cleansed our hearts, souls, and minds
by wandering the barren deserts of negative Christianity, let's begin to
wade across the turbulent waters of our economy and allow the Bible to positively shape us for a new day in a new land.

We might begin by asserting that God graciously created all wealth and
still owns that wealth. God then created humankind with the ability to par-
ticipate in this creative process. Since that day, the Garden—or an economy
where God, not humanity, determines what is good and what is evil—has
been as ripe a field as any for the creative endeavors of God's children.

Taking the Bible seriously does not mean we should slavishly adhere to
every economic principle found in the Bible, particularly some of the more
legalistic ones in the early part of the Old Testament, as few of us live in an
arid land of subsistence agriculture. To do so would be to fall prey to what
theologians call "biblicism." Contemporary theologians commonly view
many of the Old Testament's economic laws as most Christians view its
dietary laws, that is, as enriching principles to be considered, rather than as
binding absolutes that must be obeyed.

It is the loving spirit of the Bible—and not the meaning of specific verses addressed to an ancient people—that frees us for the more abundant life in our modern world. From my perspective, the Bible's message in the area of economics can be broken down into six broad themes or principles:

1. *Having faith, not fear.* Noting that God had blessed the eternally-minded Abraham for choosing brotherhood over expanded territory in the short run (Genesis 13:8–15), Moses and other patriarchs decried fear and the political, economic, and psychological bondage it produces among the spiritually immature. They often preached, "Fear not," promising that if faith were to replace fear, the community of God would find the freedom to prosper.

2. *Seeking communal abundance, not individual riches.* As many "prosperity theologians" do today, many later Israelites, including Job's friends, turned the assurance of *communal* blessings into a guarantee of *personal* riches. Notice that even as Moses promised material blessings to the nation for its faithfulness, he realistically made adequate provision for the poor individuals who will be with us always.

3. *Praying for righteousness, not riches.* Solomon observed the paradoxical nature of spiritual wealth creation when he prayed for wisdom but received wealth as well. God thereby established priorities for God's people, who too often erroneously go directly for the wealth without bothering with the discipline. Solomon also recognized that material wealth does not fill that God-shaped hole in the heart of every spiritual being.

4. *Giving hearts, not money.* Greed had replaced fear as the primary concern of both the major and minor prophets. While this would likely never occur in a modern church or ministry, true prophets often *rejected* the offerings of the people as the people sought to sacrifice a bit of money for all their hearts, souls, and minds.

5. *Seeing the poor as rich.* Jesus and his followers noticed that the pagan Romans often slept in palaces while Jesus had no place to lay his head. Knowing that many of his disciples were destined to sleep in cave-like catacombs, Jesus declared the reality that God graciously "makes it to rain on the just and unjust," thus moderating,

though not repudiating, the direct correlation of faith and material riches.

6. *Being content.* The apostle Paul shared the great secret that true spirituality produces contentment, whether we have little or much. In a similar vein, he appeals for "moderation in all things."

If any biblical principles should be highlighted or emphasized by a Christian author, they should be those paradoxical principles taught by Christ, who is the focal point of the Christian faith. "Seek first the kingdom," Jesus said, "and all this shall be added unto you." He knew that fear, greed, impatience, and turning our finances into an entwined weed that can choke our spiritual growth have no place in the abundant life. So he counseled that love should squeeze those negative motives out of our hearts and minds.

Jesus never taught that it was unethical to earn money. He did teach the paradox that "the first shall be last," because the selfish pursuit of money can interfere with spiritual riches. This is reflected in Paul's admonition not to do *anything* from selfish ambition (Philippians 2:3), which would include creating the money that would later be given to ministry. The ethic of Jesus is symbolized by the cross, which suggests that every thought and every action should reflect the faithful love of God on the vertical dimension and a love of neighbor as self (not *instead* of self) on the horizontal dimension.

Living in a World Where Greed Is Good and Charity Is Not a Virtue

Even my most faithful clients too often fail to appreciate the extent to which Jesus' perspective stands radically opposed to the predominant values of the contemporary world. Gordon Gekko said during the 1980s, "Greed is good." Donald Trump said during the 1990s: "The point is that you can't be too greedy." Even Alan Greenspan, chair of America's Federal Reserve Board, has written: "It is precisely the greed of the businessman, or, more appropriately, his profit-seeking, which is the unexcelled protector of the consumer." The words "unexcelled protector" should give pause to those of us who put our faith in the love of God and neighbor rather than the greed of the businessman. Greenspan has also testified before Congress that we will have to live with the boom-and-bust cycles caused by fear and greed because "there is no tool for changing human nature," such as a Christmas spirit—which is the spirit of Christ—that can melt the heart of any Scrooge.

Most people I consult feel such unbiblical sentiments were simple exuberance during the great bull market of the '80s and '90s. They are very wrong. Without exaggeration, there is a mountaintop battle of biblical proportions occurring between the prophets of Yahweh and the prophets of mammon. The late philosopher Ayn Rand wrote to friends that she essentially wanted to establish a new religion that would be more in tune with selfish-human rather than loving divine nature. Since that required doing away with the revelations of Scripture, Rand taught "reason is the only absolute" and that traditional "faith is a malignancy." Christ taught that a more abundant life is obtained through the virtue of keeping our neighbor's interests at least on the same level as our own, particularly the interests of the "least of these." Rand taught that humanity's "self-interest can be served only by a non-sacrificial relationship with others." In a now famous interview, she told *Playboy* that charity is not a virtue, much less an obligation. Her book *The Virtue of Selfishness* is still quite popular with the business and intellectual set, who do not seem to consider that Rand died depressed and virtually alone.

Ms. Rand, as well as we modern witting or unwitting disciples who are increasingly suffering from depression and anxiety, might have found a more balanced and abundant life had she had the benefit of this counsel from British philosopher Anthony O'Hear, as expressed in *After Progress: Finding the Old Way Forward:*

> When people were religious . . . they sought and often found fulfillment in self-forgetfulness. They looked to God, or their family, or their vocation or their craft, rather than to themselves. Psychology becomes central in a society only when people forget God or lose any sense of their allotted roles and identity. This explains why, in our century, psychology and associated therapies have replaced religion and tradition as guides as how to live, and why more and more of us seek counseling of various sorts as the answer to our problems and why the domain of the mentally disturbed grows ever larger.

Alan Greenspan, often described as the most powerful economic player in the world, literally sat at Rand's feet each day for several years. Ms. Rand then sat in the front row at the White House when he was sworn in as head of our nation's monetary system. Junk bond king Michael Milken, Arnold

Schwarzenegger, and other very influential celebrities are among the disciples of her teachings. A major *USA Today* article on September 24, 2002 said America's corporate scandals had sent our corporate leaders scurrying to dust off her book *Atlas Shrugged.*

The article added that *Atlas Shrugged* had been voted by Book of the Month Club members as the second most influential book after the Bible. That could be a metaphor for America, since *Atlas Shrugged* ended with Rand's new humanistic savior making a new sign over the world that would take the place of the cross. It was the sign of the dollar. If that sounds far-fetched, ask yourself why you work where you do; why you invest where you do; and what you think of most often during any day except Sunday. (Psychologists tell us that people think about money more than they think about sex!) Do we invest our time, talent, and treasure where we love God and neighbor as self, or where we can make the most money?

Rabbi Michael Lerner has noted:

> There's nothing wrong with free trade and a free market, as long as they operate within the context of a world governed by God—a world in which the bottom line of money and power is subordinate to the higher bottom line of love, caring, ethics, and ecological sensitivity, as well as awe and wonder and a celebration of creation. The problem happens when the "realistic" subordinate ethical and spiritual values and make free trade into a modern idol to be worshipped above all other values—and when they tell us that anything else is "unrealistic."

Mennonite economic theologian Dr. James M. Harder maintains:

> When historians write their accounts of the late twentieth century, a significant theme—perhaps the *most* significant theme—will be "economism." Coined only a decade ago by process theologian John B. Cobb, Jr., the term economism has come to symbolize an increasingly dominant belief that the single most important value to modern society is economic growth. Cobb himself strongly condemns what he perceives to be the "idolatry" of economism. "It is profoundly opposed to Christianity," he argues. "A Christian must condemn a society that organizes itself for the pursuit of wealth and encourages its citizens to order their lives this way."

The tension with Jesus' ethic is stunning, if less so than some nearly ascetic clergy assume. While some religions deny that the self exists, Christ thought it was very real. While he knew we would have to deny self completely if we are to find the greatest bliss possible—that is, the joy that the saints like Mother Teresa have known—his commandment is to simply elevate the interests of our neighbors to those of ourselves. This discipline would allow an economy to function quite well, with management, shareholders, and customers benefiting fairly. If you think a few moments about America's corporate scandals, you realize they were essentially the result of Rand's ethic trumping the ethic of Jesus.

Jesus summarized the law and prophets with the two concepts together known as the Great Commandment. It says we must first love God and then love our neighbors as ourselves if we are to achieve the abundant life. Similarly, a balanced biblical ethic of wealth creation—as opposed to simply a Jewish ethic or a Christian ethic—might be summarized in two basic concepts. First, the earlier Jewish Scriptures *primarily* counsel us to become prudent and ethical co-creators of wealth for ourselves, our neighbors, and particularly for those in need. While there is considerable overlap, the later Christian Scriptures *primarily* counsel us to avoid anxiety over the economic future and subsequently to avoid preoccupation with material well-being, rather than with the spiritual and ethical kingdom.

At first glance, those two ideas may appear to be in tension. And they do often create confusion among Christians in particular. I spend a large part of my time answering essentially the question, "How can we create abundant wealth, particularly as it is defined in America, without dwelling on it?" Yet as we have seen repeatedly throughout the past two decades, anxiety is a primary deterrent to creativity in every sphere of economic, political, and spiritual life. Financially, I can only assure you that some of my happiest clients have invested simply in a prudent and ethical mutual fund, forgotten about it, and thought of more important matters.

Creating a Christian Culture Where Money Becomes the Root of Much Good

"Wealth and enterprise have so woven themselves around the message of Jesus that popular models of Christianity appear as nothing more than self and greed at the center, with strands of Christian thought at the periphery." —Ravi Zacharias

The church has a very long way to go in its efforts to again understand and apply a holistic biblical ethic in the economic arena. Not only do many clergy not know *how* to preach an economic sermon; many don't even know *why* they should. The answer to that why is rooted in the fact that economics was a favorite topic of Moses, Solomon, Jesus, and Paul as it acknowledges dominion. Many preachers have reminded us that the love of money is the root of all evil, but not enough have explored the ramifications of money being the root of much good, especially outside that box we call the church.

A national survey conducted by the Lutheran Brotherhood (now known as Thrivent Financial) concluded that fully one-half of surveyed Lutherans think it is "inappropriate to discuss money and material possessions at their place of worship." At the same time, most of those surveyed didn't know that money and the things it can buy are the most frequently discussed topics in the Bible. Only two percent of respondents cited money as a common biblical subject. This is a startling fact as the Evangelical Lutheran Church in America (ELCA) is one of our more affluent and supposedly financially enlightened denominations.

Very few clergy are taught anything about money in seminary or in their continuing education. Therefore, they are only vaguely aware that mammon and the tithe are simply opposite sides of the same coin, or that money is morally neutral. St. Augustine said: "Avarice is not a fault inherent in gold, but in the man who inherently loves gold, to the detriment of justice." So, pastors typically view money as a rather tarnished subject, one that more "worldly" employees and volunteers, such as church boards and fundraisers, will address. This is a dualistic rather than holy worldview.

Meanwhile, so-called stewardship conferences typically dwell *exclusively* on funding our churches and ministries. Unfortunately, writing and talking exclusively about giving and misnaming it "stewardship" can actually *prevent* church members from understanding the holistic nature of stewardship advocated in Scripture. Avoiding economics is near gnosticism.

Again, a holistic approach defines abundance in terms far broader than mere money. The paradox is that seeing the larger reality may help us to see more money in the future. Economists like to think of the world as one big pie. They think about how large the pie is and how to make it even larger in the future. Politicians often focus on whether most citizens are getting an "equal" or "just" slice of the pie. These considerations are important, but not as important as the question Jesus asked, which is essentially: "What does it profit you to gain a nice share of a larger pie if it contains soured ingredients and doesn't taste as sweet as it should?" The point is that we can't separate our economic and political lives from our morality and spirituality. As someone has said, even a train wreck increases this year's GNP as the train and track are put back together. Unfortunately, it may not enrich us in the long run because what is spent cannot be spent on a new train for another track.

Thinking tactically for the short run will do little to enrich the institutional church. We must begin thinking strategically for the long run. During most of the 1990s, I attended the ecumenical stewardship meetings of the National Council of Churches. Each year, the goals for the next year were, first, to fund the financial crisis in the mainline churches, and second, to teach holistic stewardship in our colleges and seminaries. When I attended similar evangelical conferences, no one even pretended to be concerned with the second goal. Very few in either group seemed to realize that we will never adequately fund our moral institutions until we help people understand what Jesus was getting at when he said: "Seek first the kingdom and all this will be added unto you," even if you work in a church.

Unfortunately, the vast majority of churches fails to distinguish between fundraising and financial ministry. Fundraising focuses on the needs of the church, while financial ministry focuses on the needs of the church's members, their neighbors, their environment, and so on. Ironically, it usually happens that when a church serves the needs of others, such as its members and those in need, it is more likely to be blessed financially in miraculous ways.

Robert Wuthnow, who heads the Center for the Study of American Religion at Princeton University, states in his book *The Crisis in the Churches: Spiritual Malaise, Fiscal Woe:*

> The steady drop in donations, volunteering, and personal involvement is a direct result of a spiritual crisis—a crisis caused in large part by the clergy's failure to address the vital relationships between faith and money. . . . The solution is *not* simply to talk more about the financial needs of the church— 30 percent [of survey respondents] said they would actually give less money if the churches talked more about finances than they now do. The answer is to talk about the broader relationships between faith, work, money, giving, the poor and economic justice.

Nonordained disciples of Christ must similarly develop a more integrated and holistic view of their financial responsibilities. A concept advanced by Bob Buford, a popular Christian author and the prosperous owner of a television network, illustrates the problems that occur when the laity receive no help in these matters. In his book *Half-Time*, Buford, whom I consider a friend, essentially coaches businesspeople who are approaching or mired in midlife crisis to make a transition "from success to significance." That someone can achieve success without achieving significance suggests that even we in the church are now defining success primarily in financial terms.

"Half-time" refers to the idea that we can basically spend the first half of our careers making money and the second half using it for meaningful causes. It's a helpful concept for those baby boomers who have neglected their spiritual lives. But it can also unfortunately validate the notion that we can compartmentalize our business ventures from faith. We can end up preaching one message through our businesses and a diametrically opposed message in our ministries. The April 13, 2002 edition of *The Economist* observed in a special survey of television: "There are few social phenomena, pernicious or benign, for which television is not being held responsible by someone or the other; the stifling of children's imagination, the increase in obesity, the decline of the family meal, the erosion of morality, the vulgarization of taste, the worship of celebrity, the promotion of violence, the undermining of authority . . . "

More responsible activities on the part of television, particularly religious television, may be especially important during coming decades. My friend Professor Roland Miller, who lived among Muslims for twenty-five years as he became one of the West's leading authorities on their faith, has written in *Muslim Friends*: "There are three factors that have made it harder for non-Muslims to view Muslims as persons. . . . Superficiality represents a common dilemma of our time related to the 30–second clip approach of TV knowledge. That gives us the sense of learning and not its substance, resulting in a kind of stick-figure imagery. Moreover, the great abundance of various materials makes us rather content with what we receive, since we have neither the time, energy, or patience to delve more deeply into the labyrinth of issues that confront us. Muslims, with others, suffer from this process. Dealing superficially with fellow human beings trivializes them, and frequently warps their reality. To understand the reality of Islam means to penetrate beneath these surface impressions to the deeper levels of Muslim faith and emotion."

As a board member of Robert Schuller's *Hour of Power*, which is broadcast internationally each Sunday morning, I know that it's possible to use television in a positive way. But I also know what the authors of *Christianity Incorporated* meant when they wrote: "Both together and separately, television and advertising/marketing represent two of the most powerful means of human formation [what we might call habits of the heart] in our world. If we are to gauge adequately the degree of conflict between capitalist and Christian formation, we must look at how the world of commerce and the world of faith shape human affections, dispositions, and practices; doing so will illustrate the extent to which the formative practices of the for-profit culture industries triumph over the cultivation of Christian ways of being in the world." Doing so will also illustrate why the biblical ethic clearly suggests that Christians need to find significance *in* our careers, not *after* them or *outside* them in our part-times, by integrating our faith with all that we do. That is, our success must become our significance.

A more holistic ethic in the area of finances is built in part on what Sir John Templeton refers to as an "attitude of gratitude," which the Bible says comes from counting our blessings. Sir John then always taught the financial planners who sold his funds that they were "ministers" when they put their clients' interests first. He then walked his talk by never using his great wealth for a huge house, multiple residences, yachts, and private planes. Even today, he flies coach because he has always believed and taught that the back of the plane gets there at the same time as the front of the plane. He simply finds his greatest joy in using any wealth that God entrusts to his care to build more godly hearts, minds, and souls, which the Bible defines as the spiritual kingdom that can then shape a more prosperous world, rightly defined. For decades John Templeton has celebrated Thanksgiving Day so he can keep Christmas spiritual.

This attitude carries over into his investment philosophy. While many media celebrities focused millions on the negatives of the federal debt during the early nineties, Sir John focused on the positive side of America's balance sheet and the incredible value of our assets. (Although I asked constantly, I never found one person who knew America's assets were valued at $55 trillion when tens of millions were paranoid over our $5 trillion federal debt.) In his most recent appearance on the cover of *Forbes*, Sir John explained to

readers "how to beat the market." He said that the way to prosper is to buy
when others have lost hope and their low spirits are reflected in low stock
prices. The corollary is to sell when others are euphoric and their too-high
expectations are reflected in too-high stock prices. If you think it through, not
only is that good for our finances, it is good for our neighbors. To use an agricultural analogy, we plant when there are shortages due to others' failure to
plant but don't when there is excess due to excess planting or investment.

Such an approach is counterintuitive to base human nature. There is psychological security in planting when our neighbors are. But, the other
approach has been valid since ancient times. One of the earliest Old Testament accounts tells us that the time to build an ark is when most people are
so focused on the streams of riches that flow during the good times that
they can't see the clouds building on the horizon. The same story tells us to
watch for olive branches just when the waters seem the deepest. Another
biblical story tells us that seven good years are followed by seven lean years.
Jeremiah bought his field when the future looked bleak. And so on.

Being able to discern when humankind is caught up in either fear or greed
requires spiritual insight and the acknowledgement that, absent the Christ
spirit, human nature is weak, not heroic or perfectly rational as many economists believe. It also takes the spiritual maturity and perspective of Jeremiah
to remain hopeful of the future when others have grown hopeless and believe
the end is near. And, it requires the wisdom of Solomon.

After the Bible, Sir John Templeton's favorite investment book may be
Extraordinary Popular Delusions and the Madness of Crowds. It too helps us
to understand that prudence is simply a moderation of the fear and greed
that dominate humankind from time to time.

Despite this being profoundly spiritual, the Christian culture has received
little help toward developing more positive disciplines in the financial arena.
"Thou shalt not run up thy credit cards" or "Thou shalt not enjoy a new car"
or most particularly, "Thou shalt not forget to tithe" are just a few of the
negative legalisms. As a board member of several cash-intensive ministries,
I deeply appreciate how consumerism and debt can divert resources from
potentially higher spiritual uses. Yet negative legalisms still reflect poorly on
the positive and creative spirit of the biblical ethic.

Despite all the guilt Christendom can lay on spending money, the West-
minster Shorter Catechism reminds us that it is a "chief end" of humankind

not only to "glorify God" but to "enjoy him forever." We should never confuse the enjoyment of God with the enjoyment of God's gifts. St. Augustine wrote: "Every human evil or vice consists in seeking to enjoy things that are to be used and to use things that are to be enjoyed." In essence, the sin of prosperity theologians is in using God so they can enjoy things. But even spending should be joyful as a "lesser end," just as it was when the ancients were told by the prophets to spend generously on great feasts. Spending can be joyful again once we master the difficult art of discerning the differences between the needs, wants, and desires of the human heart. That requires a spirituality that can slip the gravity of material things.

My web site uses the angel-like butterfly to symbolize the new life in the biblical spirit and ethic of wealth creation. Some theologians believe the butterfly is actually an older Christian symbol than the far better known fish. But there is a very human reason that you seldom see the butterfly on cars and t-shirts. While the fish is a symbol of our desire to *evangelize others* into the spiritual kingdom, the butterfly implies that through *discipleship* we can gradually shed *our own* cocoons of fear, insecurity, greed, entangling complexity, and impatience in order to *grow* spiritually into the more angelic creatures that God intended mature Christians to be.

This has stewardship dimensions that are far more important than simply helping us to build larger portfolios. Fishers have to devote considerable time, talent, and treasure to the pursuit of fish. But butterflies *attract* people by simply being graciously beautiful once they shed their protective but ugly weavings and grow vulnerable to the realities of life. This more positive approach was advocated by an insightful editorial Michael Novak wrote for *The Wall Street Journal*:

> As the world enters the third millennium, we may hope that the church, after some generations of loss of nerve, rediscovers its old confidence in the economic order. Few things would help more in raising up all the world's poor out of poverty. The church could lead the way in setting forth a religious and moral vision worthy of a global world, in which all live under a universally recognizable rule of law, and every individual's gifts are nourished for the good of all. . . . The current tendency of many to base the spirit of capitalism on sheer materialism is a certain road to economic decline. Honesty, trust, teamwork and respect for the law are gifts of the spirit. They cannot be bought.

Many theologians believe that the apostle Paul collected money all over the Mediterranean for the early church in Jerusalem because it was in economic depression. Christians erroneously thought there was no need to invest for the future since Christ was returning shortly. I watched as many Christians did the same during Desert Storm, federal budget deficits, and the millennial madness of the 1990s. Some continue to do so today and fail to see that their view of the future is a self-fulfilling prophecy.

In contrast, the biblical ethic calls for us to live with hope today, as opposed to being defeated by someone's prediction of a dismal future. Henri Nouwen has observed, "A man or woman without hope in the future cannot live creatively in the present. The paradox of expectation is that those who believe in tomorrow can live better today." And when Martin Luther was asked what he would do if he knew Christ was returning tomorrow, he replied that he would plant a tree today. Or as Gandhi put it, "If we will take care of today, God will take care of tomorrow."

Expanding Our Sense of Stewardship to Social Responsibility

The biblical ethic clearly indicates that taking care of today includes being conscious of what we are investing in for tomorrow. Unfortunately, while I know of few Christians who actually want to support such business endeavors as adult literature, cigarettes, and casino gambling, I know a large number who do so unwittingly.

I was once asked by an employee at Focus on the Family to review the mutual fund options in her retirement plan. In so doing, I discovered that Focus was essentially using some ministry contributions unwittingly to finance casino gambling companies, even as it was using other donated dollars to lobby Washington to reduce the spread of casino gambling. That's another pretty good metaphor for American Christianity today.

By and large, the financial leaders of the evangelical wing of Christianity have ignored the topic of socially responsible investing. Concerns in this area go far beyond refusing to support immoral causes. They also address our need to bring relief and healing to a world in need. Nobel laureate in economics Robert Fogel notes in his book *The Fourth Great Awakening* that half of the world's population exists on three dollars a day or less, while one-fifth of the world's population, or 1.3 billion people, survives on one dollar a day or less. *The Economist* has detailed: "One-half of sub-Saharan Africa's six hundred million people live on just 65 cents a day, and recently they have been getting poorer."

I know that every American feels pressed by bills for all those things we all "need." But even those "poor" Americans at the official poverty line consume nearly twenty times what those 1.3 billion people do.

The United States thinks of itself as a generous nation. Most Americans think that foreign aid is a major item in our government's budget. But Harvard professor Jeffrey Sachs has estimated that the average American is asked to pay only four dollars per year to aid the world's poorest 600 million people. Economic publications tell us that America gives just one-tenth of 1 percent of its enormous income in official foreign aid. That is the lowest of all major nations.

It is not my task to advocate more official foreign aid. But Americans might find greater meaning and purpose in life, and therefore become happier—perhaps slowing the epidemic of anxiety and depression in the U.S.—if we grow more conscious of our blessings and lovingly share them with our neighbors suffering from other epidemics. As we invest 1 percent of our wealth in the community development banks that fight domestic poverty, we might invest another 1 percent in a "developing markets" mutual fund. Small as that might seem to us—and it's far less than we invested in worthless Internet companies at the beginning of the new millennium—that amount of money could play a huge role in improving the material condition of Africa and other poor areas around the world.

Some persons of influence have advanced the notion that socially conscious and responsible investing is very difficult, if not impossible. Austin Pryor, a regular on Larry Burkett's radio show and on the Moody radio network, has written in his newsletter titled *Sound Mind Investing:*

> I receive more questions on ethical investments than on any other single topic. I believe the people writing have a genuine desire to please and glorify the Lord in every aspect of their lives, including their finances. They sincerely strive to be faithful stewards, and believe they have a responsibility to be sure they do not lend economic support to those worldly forces in opposition to what they see as biblical values. I respect their heartfelt concerns. Unfortunately, I must tell them I can be of no help. Why not? Because I know of no

investments that are guaranteed to meet their criteria. There are no righteous investments. . . . I want to encourage you to shift your thinking away
from boycotting the purchase of a company's stock (which has no potential
to bring about change) toward boycotting the purchase of their goods and
services (which has proven quite effective in changing behavior).

Similarly, during the 1990s, investment advisor and author Ron Blue sent
a form letter to clients inquiring about socially responsible investing. It
stated, "it is virtually impossible to monitor morality and ethics...." As Pryor
also indicated, the letter went on to explain that even if you put your money
in a bank certificate of deposit, the bank might do something objectionable
with it. The exercise in moral relativism did not explain that is precisely why
many responsible investors put some of their money in "community development banks" which finance affordable housing and churches for the poor,
thereby creating meaningful jobs and hope rather than welfare and government dependence.

It is probably true that there are no "righteous" investments. After all, corporations, banks, and insurance companies are made up of people, and the
Bible teaches that there are no perfect people. But theologians know that
our inability to achieve moral perfection should not keep us from striving to
do the best we can in any area of life.

I know from experience that socially conscious investors *can* make meaningful progress toward their goals. And I know that there are more than financial rewards for doing so. During the past decade, I have invested more of
my own and my clients' resources in ethical mutual funds that finance generally beneficial wealth creation for Americans and those in other nations.
Not only have I avoided the huge losses associated with recent corporate scandals, I *found myself*—hopefully the true self that God intended—at conferences filled with thousands of kindred spirits. I've invested in prudent mutual
funds that finance basic infrastructure such as electrical plants and telephone
companies in developing nations, and *found myself* talking with the government and business leaders of Uganda at the request of the Church of England.
In Uganda, whose moral foundations of political economy were being rebuilt
after being destroyed by Idi Amin, I *found myself* as enriched by the unshak-
able faith and joyful spirituality of African Christianity as they were by my
explanation of the role of the biblical ethic in democratic capitalism.

I have also invested my son's education fund in the South Shore Bank of Chicago, an inner-city bank that uses investors' money to rehabilitate afford-able housing for the poor, and *found myself* sleeping better knowing I had played a role in defusing future racial tensions among our children and their neighbors. (Some of my friends laughed at my 5 percent as they bought Internet stocks!) Very simply, by considerable trial and error, I have discov-ered the enriching wisdom of Jesus' teaching that we should "make friends for yourself with worldly wealth" (Luke 16:9). That kind of selfishness is indeed a virtue.

For those of us with a little more money than we need at the moment—which is a pretty good definition of an investor—no wisdom or reality could make us richer, either spiritually or financially. What's more, I have discov-ered that investments of treasure in a moral and ethical way not only produce competitive, if not superior, financial rewards but perhaps as much meaning and joy as my philanthropic investments in churches, colleges, and charities.

The typical mutual fund manager or financial writer argues that ethics must cost us money. That is, ethical investments don't produce lucrative results. Sir John Templeton has always taught the exact opposite. He believes that true biblical ethics often sift out companies that will eventually run into trouble with regulators, health agencies, pressure groups, and labor organi-zations. For that reason, Sir John always avoided companies primarily engaged in the support of alcohol, tobacco, gambling, adult literature, and other moral and social ills. As the Dean of Global Investing, John virtually pioneered the concept that even small investors in wealthy nations might invest in the well-being of their neighbors around the world.

❧

By now, I hope you have begun to think differently about the relationship between Christian faith and your financial life. The remainder of this book consists of short commentaries on Bible passages, some often ignored; com-mentaries that hopefully represent the holistic spirit and ethic of the Bible. Read them in the spirit in which Jesus undoubtedly read them in their orig-inal context. He was serious when he said, "As long as heaven and earth last, not the least point nor the smallest detail of the Law will be done away with"

(Matthew 5:18). Yet he also understood the Law to be simple snapshots of how people might live once their hearts, minds, and souls were set afire by the gracious and loving spirit of God.

As you read the remaining chapters in this book, remember that they are largely wise counsel that I have found enriching. Relatively few are absolute because God's loving spirit does not bind us but frees us to move beyond our comfort zones to think, feel, and eventually live in a different way. While that spirit always loves us just as we are, it also loves us far too much not to help us grow even richer by maturing in wisdom and grace. Like the butterfly pressing to escape the cocoon, we can't be the beautiful creatures God intended if we don't mature.

As the first step can be frightening for even a butterfly, we could do worse than to take flight with these words from the Rev. Dr. Peter Gomes in *The Good Book*: "When we read the Bible, we do not know all that we need to know. We do not know all that 'they' knew. We do know, however, that what we have is what they have left to us, and that translating that treasure from their time into ours and back again is an enterprise that calls for patience, endurance, skill and perhaps above all humility."

Be assured that when you finish, you'll understand that even the saints have treasured God's mysteries as dearly as God's revelations. Humbly accept and treasure both.

Part II

The Ethic of the Jewish Scriptures

❧

"In Judaism, wealth is seen as both a blessing and as a responsibility. The wealthy are expected to share their blessings with others and to be personal role models of social and communal responsibility: *Richesse oblige*. To a considerable extent, that is what happened in most Jewish communities at most times, and it is what saved Jews from the decadence associated with affluence. . . . Jewish teaching is best summarized in the famous aphorism of Hillel: 'If I am not for myself, who will be? But if I am only for myself, what am I?' Judaism is personal responsibility allied with social responsibility."

Rabbi Professor Jonathan Sacks

CHAPTER FOUR

THE CREATIVITY OF THE PATRIARCHS

"In a sense, God took five days to create the universe, and on the sixth day named humans as his agents to continue the creative process. Thus economics—from the Greek word *oikonomia*, meaning stewardship— viewed from a creational aspect would be carrying out the perfect will of God in developing his creation to ever-higher stages of goodness . . . furthering God's plan by seeking to bring out his goodness in every aspect of life."

Charles (Chuck) Colson; Christian author and apologist
Recipient, the Templeton Prize

❧

In the beginning, God created . . .

(GENESIS 1:1)

T HIS BOOK primarily focuses on a biblical ethic of wealth creation (not *the* biblical ethic, but *a* biblical ethic, which I believe is needed in the West at this point in history). It focuses on wealth *creation* because when the Western church discusses money today, it typically quotes Bible passages about wealth *redistribution* through tithing, giving, estate planning, taxation, Third World debt forgiveness, and so on. If you ask any church leader what "stewardship" is, he or she is likely to reply that ideally it means giving 10 percent to ministry. As Christians always fall short of the ideals taught, that's probably why church members settle for giving 2 percent. Yet stewardship in the biblical spirit is far more about how we co-create and co-manage with God and our neighbors *all* wealth than it is about how we share a small portion of our *incomes*.

Ironically, an exclusive focus on giving, as legitimate and important as that may be to the institutional church, can actually *prevent* people from understanding the holistic nature of biblical stewardship. As the U.S. Catholic bishops confessed in their stewardship pastoral letter titled "Stewardship: A Disciple's Response" a few years ago: "Concentrating on one specific obligation of stewardship, even one as important as church support, could make it harder—even impossible—for people to grasp the vision." So, if you believe you understand stewardship, I would ask you to repeat after me, "Stewardship is not exclusively about giving to religious institutions." You may need to say it several times.

In essence, the responsibility for wealth *creation* has become centered in the somewhat more secular institutions such as Wall Street, our banking systems, the financial media, and our business schools. I say "somewhat" more secular because most Americans are not aware of the many devoutly religious figures who can be found in these institutions. While these persons may not always subscribe to the idea that faith can influence all our assets, some may understand better than most pastors, seminarians, and particularly stewardship officers the biblical concept that wealth must be created before it can be shared.

The reduction of the biblical ethic from holistic wealth management to the giving of a one-fifth tithe is a serious problem for the relevance of the institutional church to our money culture, particularly in the area of evangelism. Jesus often used the language of material wealth to teach spiritual principles, because people who knew little about spirituality could relate other values to material wealth. As we will see, he said things such as, "The kingdom of heaven is like a coin, a pearl," and so on. Ironically, in our own ministries, we tend to use spiritual language in the world and expect those immersed in material culture to understand our language. Jesus pointedly and accurately said that our own hearts will always be where our treasure is (Luke 12:34). *He did not say our hearts will be where our tithing and giving are.* He knew that our treasure is far more than the tithe and far more than the average 2 percent Americans give largely to ourselves—for the comfort and convenience of nicer church buildings, air conditioning, and so on.

Christ's church should be conscious of the deep implications of his teaching. Otherwise, 98 percent of our incomes and 100 percent of our treasure—and hearts—will remain in the material culture of the world, hardly encouraging Christians to transform it. For example, can our hearts truly be concerned about the spread of adult literature and casino gambling when our retirement investments are profiting from *Playboy* and Caesar's World even though we are tithing to ministries fighting the spread of adult literature and gambling?

Ironically, the church's myopic focus on giving probably harms the finances of the church quite seriously. There's an old saying that people give to what blesses their lives. We've all heard of patients who give their life savings to the hospital that gave them a few more days of life. And Americans who have grown wealthy typically give far more to the colleges that prepared them for the wealth-creating activities of business than they give to churches that are constantly seeking wealth redistribution.

A lighthearted saying illustrates my point well. Perhaps you've heard that it's difficult to remember your objective was to drain the swamp when you're surrounded by alligators? In essence, our religious institutions feel they're surrounded by alligators, as pastors and capital campaign consultants fight off the increasing demands that threaten to devour them and their stagnant resources. Thus very few are dedicating much time, talent, and treasure to draining the swamp by teaching a holistic ethic of wealth creation and management. Paradoxically, however, the only way to make the alligators go away permanently *is* to drain the swamp.

As we continue our journey, I hope you will understand that paradoxes such as "The first shall be last" and "Seek first the kingdom and all this shall be added unto you" are the biblical understanding of deepest reality. I don't believe that reality can ever be confused or irrational. And I believe we can adequately understand God and salvation through Christ. But, our understanding of ultimate realities—and particularly of mundane realities such as the stock market, federal debt, and Y2K—can never be complete since the human mind is limited.

That humbling fact is so important to the Christian ethic that it's worth taking a moment to see how some of our finest minds have expressed it over the centuries. The Scriptures say that God's thoughts are not always our thoughts. Augustine famously said: "Since it is God we are speaking of, you do not understand it. If you could understand it, it would not be God."

Thomas à Kempis' final words in *The Imitation of Christ* were: "If the works of God were such that they might be easily comprehended by human reason, they could not rightly be called marvelous or unspeakable." C. S. Lewis observed, "The command, after all, was 'Take, eat'; not 'Take, understand.'" Or as Marilyn Chandler McEntyre summarized the concept for our generation in the June 11, 2001 issue of *Christianity Today:*

> The outright bafflement of the disciples must itself seem baffling to those who rest comfortable in the belief they "know" the Lord on such intimate terms that they need only ask themselves "What would Jesus do?" to arrive at an immediate solution to any moral dilemma. How is it, I wonder, that they're so sure they know what Jesus would do? The very disciples who followed him around appear to have been regularly taken by surprise. What Jesus did was most often characterized by *counterintuitive,* jolting, baffling, puzzling, or unconventional moves that even his closest followers seemed unable to predict or interpret. (In particular, notice the word "counterintuitive." Successful investing is often nothing more than buying when your intuition says sell, and selling when your intuition says buy.)

That reality presents two problems for Christian authors such as myself. First, our publishing houses would obviously like for us to write books that make sense to a wide population. Unfortunately, as we have seen, studies tell us that while most American Christians are not stupid, they are biblically ignorant. Wall Street studies reflect the same ignorance in the average citizen concerning finances. So, while such statistics may tempt me to "dumb down" the ideals and wisdom of Holy Scripture and my lessons from the Street in order to reach the majority, I prefer to take the risk that you may not understand everything found here. My second problem is that, to truly present the gospel, I have to discuss topics that make all of us, including myself, quite uncomfortable. Be assured that I personally hope to remain faithful to only a portion of the ideals you are about to read. I pray that is not hypocrisy so much as a simple recognition of my very human condition.

The challenge is, perhaps, even greater for evangelical authors and publishers, for whom a defining characteristic of their evangelicalism is "certainty of belief." In short, that means we can know without a shadow of a doubt that our salvation is assured through true belief in Jesus Christ. Even accepting that (and many evangelicals may be far less confident on Judgment Day), I realize I should be quite careful not to extend that evangelical certainty into more mundane areas; for it's never fine to usurp God's omniscience since that is idolatry. In short, true religion may be a bit like marriage and parenthood. I know enough about my wife and son to love them dearly. But, I will never understand either completely. Paradoxically, my wife's mysteries only add to her allure and my son's teenage eccentricities only make him more interesting.

Then God commanded, "Let there be light"—and light appeared.
God was pleased with what he saw. Then he separated the light from
the darkness, and he named the light "Day."

(GENESIS 1:3–5)

Each day is a gift from God. That's why they call it *the present*! It is also why Robert Schuller begins broadcasts of the *Hour of Power* with the words: "This is the day the Lord has made. Let us rejoice and be glad in it."

While we are primarily concerned about investing treasure, time may actually be the most important resource we invest. After all, the Federal Reserve prints more money every day. But each day that passes is gone. Generally, treasure that is lost or wasted can be regained. Time cannot.

While it's often said that "time is money," it's actually far, far more. In a very real sense, time is life itself. Those of us who work exchange precious time—as well as our talents—for money. And while most of us grow in talent and money over the course of our careers, our years must diminish. Money—and the ever-increasing medical talents it can buy—may extend our years on the earth, but the resource of time remains limited.

Fortunately, with each year of time we lose, we gain a year of experience! But, that exchange remains a difficult reality for all of us. It is so difficult that most people prefer not to think about it, and typically avoid doing so through various forms of distracting entertainment. In contrast, true spirituality always puts us in touch with reality. It never distracts or shelters us from reality, no matter how difficult that reality might seem at the moment. The paradox is that just as being aware of death makes us more appreciative of life, being conscious of the limited number of days each of us is allotted can make each day more precious. Ask anyone who has survived a potentially fatal illness!

For example, former White House chief of staff Hamilton Jordan survived a bout with cancer to write the inspiring book *No Such Thing as a Bad Day*. It reminds us that for those who have realistically faced their own mortality, there is no such thing as a bad day at work, at school, with the kids, or even in the hospital. Every day is a good gift from God. Every day is an occasion for rejoicing. Every day is a blessing that we should manage with care.

So invest at least a few hours a week at a beach, park, or window as the sun rises. Listen as all of creation, especially the birds of the air, celebrates the new day. Invest another few hours as the sun sets. Listen as all creation expresses its awe and gratitude for the day.

And, invest a few hours each week at a place of worship and repeat what you have heard all week from creation by singing to the Creator.

By the seventh day God had finished the work he had been doing . . .
(GENESIS 2:2)

Why does the ancient story tell us that God took six days to create the universe and humankind?

Whether we believe that the six days are a literal or metaphorical description of the origins of the universe, people of The Book agree that an omnipotent God could have blinked the universe into existence in a trillionth of a second. The Bible tells us that was not God's will, however. Instead, perhaps God intended to set an example for those created in God's image because God knew an impatient world would develop many speculative ways to quickly trade wealth despite the reality that true wealth creation takes time.

The trading of wealth has reached a surprising level in modern America. Most of us are involved in trading, whether we know it or not, whether we want to be or not. For example, the typical mutual fund manager now trades all our stocks each year on average. Some very popular funds trade them each three to four months on average. Then, financial publications and professionals suggest differing funds each month. So the typical mutual fund investor will trade his or her fund every two years. Thus, most of us spend our lives trading stocks, or paying someone to do so for us. But, being a short-term trader for a very long time is not the same as being a long-term investor, whether one is a mutual fund manager or a mutual fund investor.

Day trading, commodities trading, state lotteries, and the spread of casinos are but a few other results of modernity's less than patient spirit. While it may be God's plan for economic progress to speed up as the world's population does, extreme trading is typically a questionable path to spiritual and financial riches. And, each example of extreme trading may be evidence that we have drifted too far from the biblical ethic. As Alexis de Tocqueville prophesied in *Democracy in America* at the founding of our nation: "In ages of Faith, the final aim of life is placed beyond life. They do not shift from day to day chasing some new object of desire [but] when the light of faith grows dim...men think in terms of sudden and easy fortunes, of great possessions easily won and lost, and chance in every shape and form."

The Bible indicates that wealth is a blessing both materially and spiritually when we imitate God and become co-creators, rather than simple traders of wealth for ourselves and our neighbors. While that creative process may be accelerating due to improved communications and technology, various academic studies remind investors that a biblical ethic of patience is still a virtue when it comes to creating true wealth.

For now, however, simply understand that those studies indicate there is typically an *inverse* relationship between returns and trading, even before the very debilitating costs of taxes and transactional costs are considered. Patient investors also have more time and energy for more important matters of life.

Then the LORD *God planted a garden in Eden, in the East, and there he put the man he had formed. He made all kinds of beautiful trees grow there and produce good food. . . . Then the* LORD *God placed the man in the Garden to cultivate it and guard it. He told him, "You may eat the fruit of any tree in the garden, except the tree that gives knowledge of what is good and what is bad."*

(GENESIS 2:8–17)

All those trees. All that healthy fruit. And God only put one tree off limits to humankind. But, humankind was tempted to reason and/or feel that life would be more "good" without limits. After all, if all those trees and all that fruit were so good, wouldn't just a little more be even better? As Mark Buchanan has written in *Christianity Today*:

> In the Garden of Eden, the first thing the serpent did was create in Adam and Eve a sense of scarcity. The serpent's trick, then as now, is to turn this staggering abundance and gracious protection into frightening scarcity. The serpent lied and we got taken in. Now, despite the overwhelming evidence that we live amidst overflowing abundance, we always feel it's not enough. We sense it's running out.

Thousands of years later, many Wall Street professionals, including many Christian financial leaders, essentially tempt investors with the same seemingly rational argument and/or sentiment. Look at all those healthy investments out there. If they're so good, why would you limit yourself to just those? After all, wouldn't limiting your universe of possibilities surely mean you have to limit your potential gain? Isn't that only rational? Don't you just feel it!

Perhaps . . . if you look at such things from the perspective of humanity. But God understands that limiting our possibilities *ever so slightly*—and that's a key phrase for modern investors to grasp—has the paradoxical effect of making life richer. Not only do we avoid the bad fruit, but we have more room for the good fruit.

I strongly believe that this is the economic dimension of the story about the tree of knowledge. As we will discover in other areas of the Bible, God has never been opposed to us exercising human reason. We cherish the wisdom literature of Solomon. Jesus commanded us to love with heart, soul, *and* mind. But the biblical ethic has always been that human reason is limited and can therefore be assisted by the revelations of the Bible and Holy Spirit, and perhaps by the experiences of the godly who have walked this earth recently.

Dietrich Bonhoeffer was a German Christian theologian who was executed for resisting Adolph Hitler. If anyone could sense the gulf between good and evil, Bonhoeffer should have been able to because of his first-hand experiences. Yet he began his book *Ethics* by writing:

The knowledge of good and evil seems to be the aim of all ethical reflection. The first task of Christian ethics is to invalidate this knowledge. . . . Man at his origin knows only one thing: God. It is only in the unity of his knowledge of God that he knows of other men, of things, and of himself. He knows all things only in God, and God in all things. The knowledge of good and evil shows that he is no longer at one with this origin. . . . Instead of knowing only the God who is good to him and instead of knowing all things in Him, he now knows himself as the origin of good and evil. Instead of accepting the choice and election of God, man himself desires to choose, to be the origin of the election.

We believers should carefully note that Bonhoeffer goes on to explain that the primary tension between Jesus and the Pharisees was that Jesus knew only God while the Pharisees sought to know whether each and every act they, and particularly others, engaged in was good or evil. That's why Jesus never bothered to answer directly most of the Pharisees' ethical dilemmas. He simply revealed God to them and their world. The implication is that if we are in loving union with God and neighbor, the ethical dilemmas that concern many of us would not exist.

The nuance for us is that while the West's sudden interest in ethics should never drive us to judging others, slightly limiting the number of trees that *we* harvest from can be one effective way of revealing God and the truly abundant life to our money culture. For example, during the decade of the 1990s, millions of investors, including most mutual fund managers, had trouble keeping up with the Standard & Poor's 500 (S&P 500), which basically is composed of the stocks of the five hundred largest companies in America. Yet, there was another index called the Domini Social 400 Index, which essentially is the S&P 500 index without the stocks of cigarette manufacturers, casino gambling companies, alcoholic beverage manufacturers, companies that might abuse the environment, and others. Not only did this socially conscious index plant fewer harmful trees for the garden our children will live in, but it outperformed the S&P 500 by about 2 percent a year during the '90s. Recent studies indicate that this was due to two factors. First, the excluded companies were sub-par performers as a result of being subjected to lawsuits, restricting regulations, misgovernance by unethical management, and other negative influences. Second, the money that wasn't invested in them was invested in more beneficial companies.

It may seem paradoxical to the *human* mind, but we'll see that the *divine* mind has always known it is enriching to limit the universe of trees from which you choose your investments. Each day, the wisest analysts and fund managers pare down their options so only the best remain. Ethics remain one of the most effective ways to do so.

———————————— ✌ ————————————

But the Lord God called to the man, "Where are you?"
(GENESIS 3:9)

About once a week, you probably hear a skeptic (often one who has just read a media account of mass starvation in Africa, the lack of funding to combat a deadly epidemic, or the attack on the World Trade Center) ask the question, "Where was God?" But a more pertinent question might be the one God asked Adam millennia ago: "Where are you?"

Martin Hengel, an expert on early Judaism and Christianity, has written: "God calls humanity to responsibility. In our inextinguishable desire to be like God, we are hiding from the Creator and Redeemer behind all sorts of idolatry, arguments of skeptical reason, cynical nihilism, or pure thoughtlessness. We do not want to hear God's call. But his call does not therefore cease." One of the responsibilities God calls us to is that of being an ethical investor. Ironically, that responsibility can be obscured by theology.

One of the more serious debates of the Protestant Reformation was between Martin Luther and a theologian named Erasmus. In what became known as "reformed theology," Luther essentially argued that human beings can do nothing for their own salvation. It is purely a gift of God's grace. Erasmus on the other hand was more humanist, essentially arguing that humankind must play a role in the process by actually accepting God's graceful gift of transforming love. While their argument may seem like an irrelevant, top-of-the-mountain theological debate to many people, it can play a crucial role in determining your worldview. I have several friends who have taken Luther's teaching to an unintended extreme, essentially arguing that we can do nothing to save the world. So they typically act like it, counting on God to save the world while they simply wait for it to end one way or another.

On the other hand, I have friends who seem to take Erasmus's argument beyond even Robert Schuller's famous dictum that "If it's going to be, it's up to me" in their belief that they can save the world without the help of God's gracious acts. You too probably know religious leaders who seem driven to save the world during their lifetimes. They typically burn out as quickly as corporate leaders.

Typically, I, who admittedly have spent only a little informal time studying the debates between Luther and Erasmus, seek the theological middle ground and might therefore be called a "Christian humanist." While I agree with Luther that salvation on the vertical axis between God and humankind is purely an act of grace on God's part, the salvation of the world on the horizontal axis depends on us acting as a conduit to our neighbors and environment of the grace-filled love we have received.

At its foundation, that is what this book is ultimately about. I typically end my seminars with the following statement from Sir John Templeton because I believe it summarizes what the great investor really learned about life during his decades of managing time, talent and treasure:

> If we radiate love, we will receive back joy, prosperity, happiness, peace, and long life. But if we give love only to gain one of these rewards, we have not understood love. Love in expectation of any reward is not love. When we learn to radiate love, we are fulfilling God's purpose—bringing God into expression on earth.

Then the LORD *said to Cain, "Where is your brother Abel?" "I don't know," he replied. "Am I my brother's keeper?"*
(GENESIS 4:9)

To understand the biblical ethic of managing wealth, it is crucial to understand how the Greco-Roman and Judeo-Christian cultures of the ancient Mediterranean answered this ancient question of Cain: "Am I my brother's keeper?"

The Greek philosopher Plato taught that government elites should bear the responsibility for the average person's care. Roman philosophers often said the opposite: that government should get out of the way so that the strong might create great power and wealth. The Roman wealthy often financed monuments and entertainment through philanthropy, but didn't always consider it a virtue to aid their weaker brothers and sisters.

A different ethic entered the world through the not-so-powerful and not-so-rich nation of Israel. The Jewish consciousness was that *every person* was created not only with material needs but with social and spiritual needs as well. So its ethic said that *each of us*, not simply the elite powerful and wealthy, could find meaning and purpose—and subsequently joy—by lovingly assuming personal responsibility not only for ourselves but for our brothers and sisters as well, *particularly those in need.*

Those three ethics moved westward into Europe and eventually made their way into the Americas. Today, we call the Greek perspective "liberal," the Roman perspective "conservative," and the Judeo-Christian perspective "religious." So if we understand that when we use the terms "conservative Christian" or "liberal Christian," we are typically saying that we have mixed worldviews, a process theologians call "syncretism," then we might simply call ourselves "Christian" and grow of one mind and spirit.

Most of us know that Karl Marx's modern philosophy of socialism was essentially built on the ancient Greek notion that a very liberal god would have answered Cain by saying, "Not only are you not your brother's keeper; some government elite will be your keeper as well." But, modern philosopher Ayn Rand essentially assumed a very conservative god responded to Cain's question with the pagan Roman reply, "No, you are only responsible for yourself." For example, Ms. Rand told *Playboy* that she did not consider charity to be a moral duty, or even a virtue. So it's doubtful that she would have considered investing with an eye to the well-being of one's neighbor to be a virtue either. Most investors, but particularly conservative investors, consciously or unconsciously agree with her. But, as we shall see, for thousands of years, the biblical ethic has insisted that stewards should consider how their wealth affects their neighbors.

It is easy to see why most modern secularists and cultural Christians prefer the other philosophies to the biblical ethic. As humankind has demonstrated since Cain, most of us are quick to claim our rights but slow to accept our corresponding responsibilities, which are typically linked one for one. It is also easy to see why even Christians prefer to mix the parts of the biblical ethic we like with the parts of the other ethics we like. As sociologist George Barna has often said, the mixing of religions is "the preferred religion of Americans."

At first glance, the biblical ethic is simply the most demanding ethic ever created for humankind. The responsibility to love both neighbor and self appears heavy indeed. And, Catholic theologians have historically included in that responsibility "God's preferential option for the poor." The saving grace for us is that the biblical commandment to care for neighbor and self is preceded by the commandment to love God. It is that loving connection to a spiritual power higher than ourselves that allows us to carry the responsibility for neighbors, rich and poor alike, as lightly as if we were equipped with the wings of angels.

Winston Churchill said that responsibility is the price of greatness. In *Post-Capitalist Society*, Peter Drucker noted that "responsibility must be the principle which informs and organizes the post-capitalist society." Both Churchill and Drucker recognized there is no way to build a greater church, a greater society, and greater wealth without assuming greater responsibility. As our money must finance such an economy, world, and church, it must reflect that same sense of responsibility. So, the horizontal dimension of spiritual investing is "socially responsible" or "values-based" investing. Fortunately, not only does this investment strategy reflect the "neighbor as thyself" ethic, but it is the fastest-growing concept on Wall Street.

As we shall see over and over, paradoxically values-based investing may also be the most rewarding ethic for even ourselves as investors. Having said that, however, let me quickly caution as John Templeton has said: If we investors love our neighbors simply for the extra return, we have not understood love. We will not be operating within the biblical ethic. In a perverse way, we are simply more money oriented than our money culture as we are using religion for money.

Invest ethically simply because you're a reflection of a graceful and loving Creator.

The Lord said to Abram, "Leave your country, your relatives, and your father's home, and go to a land that I am going to show you."
(GENESIS 12:1)

Imagine that you have heard an unseen voice tell you to stop focusing on your family, pack up everything you have, and start walking to a foreign land. Assuming you even give such a voice a second thought, odds are good your first question would be "To where?" But Abram, later called Abraham, didn't ask. He just started his walk in faith.

Spiritual investors must typically take the same walk of faith in order to prove successful. While we may establish goals when we invest in stocks and mutual funds, we have no guarantees of where the markets will take us. When we create new businesses, we have no assurances that they will be profitable. When we create new churches and ministries, we have no idea if they will prove successful. Even when we start new families, we have little idea of what journey they will take us on.

Interestingly, as wealth grows far more intangible—that is, the land, oil, and timber that constituted most of our wealth in recent centuries is increasingly supplemented by computers and other knowledge-based industries—faith plays a far greater role in its creation. Consider this simple illustration. It is not all that difficult to look at a piece of land and visualize crops growing there. But who could have looked at the first primitive laser or computer and seen the vast wealth creation that lay ahead for those industries? George Gilder, perhaps the reigning guru of technology, wrote these words in an editorial titled "The Faith of a Futurist," published in *The Wall Street Journal* on the very first day of the new millennium:

> Imagination, intuition, and hypothesis are the first steps of technical creation. As in love, a man must trust his intuition, and act on faith, before he can really know. Love appears blind to outside observers, but lovers know that it is guided by a more exalted vision and opens new realms of knowledge and creativity. . . . We may not always describe ourselves as religious. But the act of creation is a religious act. Religious faith takes many forms,

from church attendance to prophetic visions. But they all entail a commitment to ideas or concepts that are unprovable at the outset. . . . Without religious commitment, new ideas cannot take flight and flourish, new technology cannot be projected into untilled markets, and new systems cannot be built.

The investor who never acts until the financials affirm his choice, the athlete or politician who fails to make his move until too late, the entrepreneur who waits until the market is proven—all are doomed to mediocrity by their trust in spurious rationality and their failures of faith. . . . What does it mean to say you believe in God? A minimal definition of God is an omnipotent force of goodness. The Judeo-Christian tradition upholds a faith that God is one, God is good and God will prevail. A belief in God asserts that virtue will finally triumph. No matter how dark and menacing the world seems at any particular time, goodness will win . . . These are the religious rules of economic success in millennia past, and they will obtain in millennia to come . . . An economy of ideas and innovations ultimately means an economy ruled by spirit and faith.

------------------------------ ✍ ------------------------------

Then Abram said to Lot, "We are relatives and your men
and my men shouldn't be quarreling. So let's separate.
Choose any part of the land you want. You go one way, and I'll go
another." . . . After Lot had left, the LORD said to Abram, "From where
you are, look carefully in all directions. I am going to give you
and your descendants all the land that you see."
(GENESIS 13:8–9,14–15)

Genesis 13 describes Abram as "a very rich man." Lot was also prosperous. And because they had "too many animals" for the pastureland they shared, their families and employees were in conflict. It seems that familial discord surrounding great wealth is a very old story rather than a modern soap opera!

But, Abram knew in his soul such conflict was wrong. So, in the interests of brotherhood and peace, Abram did the gracious, if apparently irrational thing. He offered Lot the first choice of the pastureland. And Lot did the seemingly rational thing. He looked for the very best land in the valley and claimed it. Abram seemed content to make do with the poorer land. But at this point the story grows interesting, for God promises to bless not rational and savvy Lot but gracious and contented Abram with the whole land and descendants too numerous to count.

And here perhaps is one of the greatest insights of the Judeo-Christian faith: True wealth, or wealth both earned and used in a righteous way, is a gift from God—*an indirect byproduct of, rather than the direct goal of, the spiritual life.* Or, as Jesus would later put it, "Seek first the kingdom and all this shall be added unto you." In a sense, it is most similar to the achievement of happiness. The more you think about making yourself happy, the more miserable you will most probably grow. It is only by denying yourself in love of God and neighbor that you will find true joy.

That's a difficult concept for most people to grasp. We tend to see reality, particularly economic reality, through the increasingly insightful means of perceptions, rational facts, nuance, and paradox. Mastering facts is tough enough. Understanding the nuances of those facts is even tougher. But paradox is the toughest of all to comprehend, even if it is deepest reality.

Trusting in the paradoxical realities of life requires considerable faith. But there have been recent studies at Ivy League business schools indicating that graduates who pursue their passions actually do better financially than graduates who pursue money itself. Case studies of corporations validate the same principle. And, there are examples of individuals such as John Templeton that indicate investors who care enough to invest in the most responsible companies make more money than investors who simply pursue the highest returns. At a deeper level of understanding, that makes sense because pursuing our passions in investments or business imbues our efforts with enthusiasm and endurance. But, most of us have never thought deeply enough about it to understand the deeper wisdom.

In an October 1993 article headlined, "Evolutionary Economics: Nice Guys Don't Finish Last," *Forbes* magazine stated, "In the real living, breathing, sweating world—as opposed to the abstract world of economists—an individual is often better off giving something to the other fellow than he would be if he looked out only for number one." Is that a modern expression of the ancient story of Abram? Yes. Is it paradoxical to the human mind, particularly to the rational mind trained by our business schools? Yes. Is it still economic reality? Yes. Is it too often forgotten or ignored by the three families of The Book as we bomb skyscrapers and foreign countries for largely economic gains? Most definitely. For since the days of Abram, God has promised the earth will eventually belong to the gracious and meek, not to the acquisitive and strong.

<hr />

Then one of the angels said, "Don't look back."...
Lot's wife looked back and was turned into a pillar of salt.
(GENESIS 19:17, 26)

<hr />

Talk to virtually any inexperienced investor, and he or she will relate a story about inevitably doing the wrong thing at the wrong time. Spend a few minutes delving into how that individual chooses investments, and odds are quite good that he or she considers the recent economic scenario and then researches all the rankings of specific investments in financial publications and newspapers. Most of the time, those charts show how terrific the investment earnings have been in the most recent quarter or year. If an investment has not done well in the recent past, it does not show up in most rankings at all.

That typically means investments enter our consciousness only *after* they've risen in value. Unfortunately, as you will find in fine print beneath each chart in a mutual fund prospectus, "past performance is no guarantee of future results." That disclaimer is essentially saying that if you want your portfolio to be worth more than a pile of salt, you might look forward rather than backward. Or at least look backward with a more eternal perspective, examining the five- or preferably ten-year track record to see how the investment performed in a different economic environment. That larger picture might help you to better see the coming five, ten, or more years.

The book *The Gifts of the Jews* says that the Jewish perception of a future that is different from the past has been identified as one of the great contributions to the world. Essentially, the book explains that the majority of the ancient world saw reality as cyclical, going nowhere. If that paradigm were reality, investors would indeed want to keep doing the same thing that has been working in the recent past. We could then make money by financing chariot manufacturers rather than car manufacturers. But, the Jewish people helped the world understand that economic reality might move toward something different in the future. It was this concept of true change that made the notion of economic progress thinkable.

Yet the Jewish people also understood the nuance that while economic progress might be somewhat linear over the long-term, there are cyclical tendencies in the short-term, such as seven fat years followed by seven lean years. That's why it is so very dangerous for investors to become fixated on what occurred in the *recent* past and, for example, jump into technology stocks as the new century began simply because they *had been* going up.

That's also why our friend John Templeton, a devout believer in long-term economic progress and a more eternal worldview, has written:

> You should resist the temptation to invest in any asset which would have produced the best performance for the previous five years. Instead, search worldwide for some type of assets which would have produced the worst performance for the past five years and then select from that list those whose depressed prices were caused not by permanent but by temporary influences.

Few investors will have the counterintuitive nature, time, expertise or discipline to do such research. But, you are more likely to hire wise people to help you with the endeavor if you recognize the need to seek people with the wisdom, experience, and vision to look forward, not those who simply ask a computer to help you look backward at recent performance.

So, while the biblical ethic endorses a look backward in order to learn from tradition, it also recommends the most "eternal" perspective possible, as we're now doing. Always remember, however, that the primary purpose of looking back on occasion is that we might see the present more clearly and thereby visualize the future with greater hope and confidence.

───────────────── ✌ ─────────────────

Every Egyptian was forced to sell his land, because the famine was so severe; and all the land became the king's property. Joseph made slaves of the people from one end of Egypt to the other.
(GENESIS 47:18–21)

Several years ago, I listened as an economically liberal theologian made the case that this story about Joseph and the famine in Egypt proves a market-based economy can't work, especially for the poor. I respect this theologian and believe his intentions were honorable, but I also believe he misunderstood the story of Joseph. For I believe Joseph was actually one of the first governmental central planners, what we might call a socialist today. With perfectly good intentions, Joseph sought to care for the people in the best way he knew how, and he was a hero in the short-term. Yet the rest of the story indicates how very seriously we must consider the consequences of our good intentions, for they might indeed pave the road to hell.

Most Christians I meet believe that after God had told Joseph to expect seven prosperous years and seven lean years, God also told him how to prepare for the economic cycle. But that belief cannot be substantiated in the Scriptures. As C. S. Lewis liked to say, when God tells us to feed the poor, God doesn't give us lessons in cooking. As much as we might appreciate a divine recipe for all of life's challenges, such as the agricultural and economic cycles of Egypt, God has honored us by creating us in the divine image instead—heart, mind, and spirit. Yet, because we are poor reflections of God's perfection, we seem to learn only by making mistakes. And a careful reading of the full story in Genesis might indicate that Joseph erred when he "collected" grain during the prosperous years but "sold" the grain back to the people during the lean years. Taking grain from the people in the interest of their future security, but requiring them to buy it back *had* to bankrupt the citizens. The point is that Joseph's well-intentioned actions on behalf of Pharaoh may actually have initiated the bondage of Egypt—and ultimately of Joseph's own people, the Hebrews. That economic mistake has been repeated throughout history, such as when Stalin essentially did the same to potato farmers to force them onto Russian collectives.

In essence, the hard lesson in reality from Egypt may be that security and freedom are on opposite ends of the spectrum of human needs. For example, Social Security has provided considerable security for older Americans in recent decades. But, by allowing the government to skim those monies off our gross income, we have given up to our "Pharaoh" the freedom to steward considerable resources in exchange for the promise of that future security.

Finding the proper balance, or political recipe, to remedy such dilemmas is a job I'll leave to discerning public servants—such as my super-capitalist friend Jack Kemp who still graciously reminded me that Joseph later "distributed" seed corn to the people—and voters. I would simply note that throughout the rest of the biblical narrative, the people of God were taught sound stewardship principles so they could steward wealth for the inevitable cycles themselves as opposed to being taught simply to shift the responsibility of wealth management to political leaders, even when assisted by well-intentioned religious leaders.

The Bible indicates there is room for both governments and markets in life. But we will surely need less government to provide for our security and basic needs when spiritual investors are again taught by religious leaders to love their neighbors as themselves in all that they do.

There in the desert they all complained to Moses and Aaron and said to them, "We wish that the LORD had killed us in Egypt. There we could at least sit down and eat meat and as much other food as we wanted. But you have brought us out into this desert to starve us to death."

(EXODUS 16:2–3)

Security or freedom? Can human beings ever decide on which side of the fence the grass is greener?

During four hundred years of slavery, the Hebrews had dreamed of freedom. But when they grew hungry during the journey to the Promised Land, they longed for the security of Egypt, even if such security came encumbered with the shackles of bondage.

In many ways, the spiritually immature Hebrews were much like teenagers, who long for the freedom to live as they like rather than as their parents feel is best, yet who still want the security of their parents' roof over their heads. Human beings only gradually give up security as we mature enough to accept the responsibilities of freedom.

In many ways, the Hebrews are also very much like the investors I deal with daily. It is no accident that Wall Street sells "securities" rather than "risks" and that our government promises social "security" rather than social "freedom." True freedom is quite frightening even to adults. That is why faith is so very crucial to life. For the paradox described in this teaching is that the only true security the Hebrews had was in the God who created them for freedom.

The same is true for investors today. Everyone wants the financial freedom that investing in stocks has produced for decades. But we also want the government guarantees of a treasury bill or CD. Some of my clients who are corporate executives and view themselves as rugged individualists grow quite insecure when they lose the security of corporate titles and benefit programs. About once a month I am approached by a broker who wants the freedom to practice investment planning the way I do. The vast majority of those brokers quickly go back to where they have been working when they discover my tiny firm can offer no security other than that freedom.

Finding the proper balance between security and freedom—or between risk and reward, to use Wall Street's language—remains the route to the investor's promised land. Finding security in God rather than wandering the deserts of human governments and corporations, and perhaps even denominations, can keep us going in the right direction.

They said to Moses, "If you speak to us, we will listen;
but we are afraid that if God speaks to us, we will die."
Moses replied, "Don't be afraid."
(EXODUS 20:20)

One of the oldest and truest sayings on Wall Street is that people make investment decisions out of fear or greed. Yet the Bible says neither of those spirits will enrich us. That doesn't keep immature investors from being primarily fearful however. While many more experienced investors appear greedy—and a few certainly are—I usually find that at a deeper level, even most of those who seem greedy, are simply afraid that they won't have enough in the future; that their government won't remain solvent to make Social Security payments; or that they don't have enough for their neighbors to consider them "successful." Those fears often manifest themselves as greed does, for each motivates the desire for more and more.

As this passage clearly indicates, fearful people usually prefer listening to human leaders rather than to God. Over and over in the Bible, God counsels faith rather than fear. But over and over, too many human leaders—unfortunately including religious leaders—raise their voices to affirm our worst fears. As earlier noted, consider the Y2K computer scare. The conservative Christian media were filled with fearful imaginings of what New Year's Day of the year 2000 might bring. When it passed without incident, I reflected again on C. S. Lewis' *Screwtape Letters*. In one particularly insightful passage, Screwtape, or Satan, instructs the young apprentice, Wormwood, concerning the subtleties of bedeviling humanity. Screwtape counsels: "There is nothing like suspense and anxiety for barricading a human's mind against the Enemy [God]. He wants men to be concerned with what they do; our business is to keep them thinking about what will happen to them."

Of course, utilizing fear as motivation is not unique to the religious media. Insurance companies often appeal to our fear of death rather than to our love of family. Some Wall Street firms play on our fear of reaching retirement without adequate savings rather than tapping our desire to finance a better life for our neighbors today. Both conservative and liberal politicians exploit our fears about Social Security's stability—conservatives to prove it unreliable and do away with it, and liberals to encourage us to shore it up with larger contributions. Yet the only thing spiritual investors should fear is being unable to hear the voice of God due to the sound of human leaders. We should never fear computer malfunctions, the U.S. government, the federal debt, or a stock market crash. We should only fear that we have grown deaf to the Voice of Love.

Too often, we hear that the "fear of the Lord" is the beginning of wisdom. That is true enough *if* we understand that fear, in the context mentioned, means "understanding." In the Great Commandment, Jesus explained that beneficial fear, or understanding, is about the *love* of God. He had this to say about the other sort of fear: "Do not be afraid; you are worth much more than many sparrows!" (Matthew 10:31) and "Courage! It is I. Don't be afraid!" (Matthew 14:27). So while the fear of the Lord may be the beginning of all wisdom, the love of the Lord is the culmination of all wisdom.

As Scripture reminds us, there is no emotional fear in love and perfect love drives out all fear (1 John 4:18). There is only rational fear, or under-standing, that God is perfect love.

If a bull gores someone to death, it is to be stoned but its owner is not to be punished. But if the bull has been in the habit of attacking people and its owner had been warned but did not keep it penned up—then if it gores someone to death, it is to be stoned, and its owner is to be put to death also.

(EXODUS 21:28)

In the modern language *Good News Bible*, this is the first verse in a section entitled "The Responsibility of Owners." It is an unparalleled, but largely ignored, section of the Bible, one that can help spiritual investors under-stand how integral the ethical is to the spiritual. A Christian's primary moti-vation arises from the vertical dimension of life, or our spiritual relationship with God, who owns the wealth we steward. But this passage reminds us that the horizontal dimension, or our relationship with humanity, is intimately connected because we are to love our fellow human beings as God has first loved us.

Despite the many rationalizations we hear for today's owners of wealth not needing to consider their neighbors, this passage is most clear how *very seri-ously* the Bible takes social responsibilities. Note that God considered it a *capital offense* for investors to *habitually* neglect those social responsibilities. There is no evidence that carelessly forgetting to tithe was of equal concern. That is because God knows that no amount of charitable giving can restore life to a neighbor who has been gored. Which is why Jesus made "love your neighbor as yourself" a dimension of the Great Commandment. The Law of Moses was realistic enough to recognize that accidents will happen in life. That's why the law graciously forgave the first careless act. But the law also emphasized God's desire for investors to be at least as conscious of the risks our investments pose to our neighbors as they pose to our own financial well-being. Then we would not be guilty of hurting people through our investments, only to give out of our surplus to heal them.

In essence, the Law of Moses made it possible for a very significant percentage of the Hebrews to manage a portion, however small, of God's wealth. But, the Law insisted that each owner of that primarily agricultural wealth should consider how his or her management of it affected the community. As we proceed, you will find that ethic applied not only to livestock, but to homes, vineyards, groves, and other forms of wealth.

In short, it was possible to see the love of God, neighbor, and self *in virtually every dimension of wealth management* in ancient Israel, *not simply in its giving and tithing.* As the wealth of Israel grew, its laws had to grow more numerous and complex, which is something investors throughout our modern world can dearly appreciate today. So, to simplify matters for humanity, Jesus spiritualized all these laws—as well as the teachings of the prophets—by simply commanding us to love our neighbors as ourselves in each and every activity of life. He went on to say that the world would then know us by our love for one another.

That is a crucial ethic for our world in the third millennium. For nearly a century, government has assumed more and more responsibility for our neighbors in need. While it is possible to argue that we're all better off materially today, it's doubtful that we're spiritually richer, or happier with corporate America and our political leaders. As author and presidential advisor Marvin Olasky has put it, "The major flaw of the modern welfare state is not that it's extravagant with money but that it's stingy with the help that only a person can give: love, time, care and hope." When spiritual investors put love, time, care, and hope into *every* financial decision, we bring our loving God into the world for all to see, and perhaps eventually love as well. What greater return could investors hope for?

If a man takes the cover off a pit or digs one and does not cover it,
and a bull or donkey falls into it, he must pay for the animal.
(EXODUS 21:33)

At the turn of the century, most Americans lived on farms. I grew up on one of those farms. Such passages about livestock management spoke very directly to most of us then. But today fewer than 5 percent of Americans live on farms. So these principles seem irrelevant to the vast majority of Americans whose wealth is increasingly in certificates of deposit (CDs), stocks, bonds, mutual funds, and real estate investment trusts, rather than in sheep, vineyards, and utilitarian wealth such as pits for burning fires, storing things, and so on.

In essence, as companies became represented by stock certificates and loans were represented by bonds and CDs, wealth has been spiritualized—rendered intangible and abstract—which makes it difficult for us to see how it's affecting our neighbors. But the primary change facing us as stewards might be that modern capitalism has separated the "ownership" of wealth from the "management" of wealth. That is, shareholders may "own" a company, but the company's management primarily decides how that company will function in our world. Investors may "own" the resources in a mutual fund, but the fund manager decides what endeavors will get financed. We may "own" the money in our banks, but a loan manager decides who gets to borrow it.

Ironically, that reality makes it both more difficult and more simple to steward resources according to the eternal principles of the biblical ethic. It's more difficult if our only goal in choosing a manager for our assets is to make as much money as possible. But, it's easier if we choose a fellow steward who understands our ethic to manage those assets.

For example, since the roaring '20s, the Pioneer Mutual Fund, managed by my Christian friend Dr. John Carey, has preferred not to invest in stocks of alcohol, tobacco, and gambling companies, or to engage in short-term speculation. Yet as mutual funds come and go on the best performing lists, Pioneer maintains a top rating from independent services. It was a member of *Forbes* magazine's Honor Roll of the top twenty funds as the millennium changed. Had you invested $10,000 in Pioneer in 1928 and suffered through the Crash of '29, the World Wars, and so on, you would have almost $70 million today, while the S&P 500 Index would have produced less than $13 million.

Because each stock in the Pioneer portfolio represents vast resources held in numerous divisions within the company, it would be quite difficult and time consuming for us to know what John Carey does when he chooses investments. But, it is a relatively simple thing to know that he is a prudent and ethical manager doing the best he can in a difficult world to manage

God's resources according to a biblical ethic. We just have to care as much about God and neighbor as money and therefore must look to an ethical manager such as John Carey to manage our funds.

———————————————— ∾ ————————————————

If you lend money to any of my people who are poor, do not act
like a moneylender and require him to pay interest.
(EXODUS 22:25)

Usury, or the earning of interest on money loaned, in business dealings with a fellow believer was officially prohibited by Christianity until the Protestant Reformation five hundred years ago. While this passage makes it seem the biblical prohibition was only against earning interest from the poor, the typical Israelite would rarely, if ever, have loaned money to those richer than himself, so the prohibition was effectively universal. Yet today, few of us worry about the biblical concept, meaning we're all basically economic progressives, or liberals. While that has created a multitude of moral and spiritual problems, I don't think lending for interest is *necessarily* bad *if* Christians remember the spirit of this Law.

The Protestant Reformation coincided roughly with the Industrial Revolution. Some historians believe the Reformation played a major role in prompting the Revolution—and therefore, in giving rise to capitalism and our higher standard of material well-being. The Reformation allowed those with money to put it into the rapidly growing banking systems rather than hoard it in the ground or under mattresses. In turn, the banks could offer loans to people who had good ideas for using money but only limited financial resources of their own. That's actually a fairly good definition of capitalism, albeit an idealistic one. As the Industrial Revolution prompted greater wealth creation in the West, there were fewer absolute "poor" in the biblical sense of barely existing from day to day. That, in turn, meant the prohibition against earning interest could be relaxed. And as wealth has grown even greater during the past century, it has been relaxed even further. Some would say too far.

Some 1.3 billion people still live on less than $1 per day, and one-half of the world's population lives on less than $3 per day. Should the biblical ethic in relation to usury still apply to them? As we will see later, there are other principles that must be considered when answering that question. But many of us believe the prohibition against earning interest from the poorest among us is still valid. So, in celebration of the new millennium, some church leaders have asked the wealthy nations to simply forgive the interest that has accrued on government to government loans made over the decades to desperately poor Third World nations, primarily in Africa. (That proposed forgiveness included the principal as well, but that is another subject covered by the Bible later.)

Some of us even believe that access to affordable credit is a moral right of individuals, as well as of governments. That is why I have long served as a board member of a Christian ministry called Opportunity International (1.800.7WE.WILL). Sir John Templeton is a spokesperson for and supporter of the same organization, along with such notable Christians as Martin Marty, Millard Fuller, and Bob Sieple of WorldVision. Opportunity International accepts charitable donations in wealthy nations and makes loans that average about $200 each to the very poor of the Third World for the purpose of job creation. (This is known as "microenterprise" or "microlending.") Loan recipients do pay interest to offset operating costs and the currency devaluations so common in Third World nations. Some conservative readers of the Bible object to even that. But the interest simply keeps the loan pools "sustainable" for future entrepreneurs who will also need to borrow. If the borrowers were allowed to repay with depreciated currency and no interest, the loan pools would quickly disappear. But more significant is that none of the wealthy donors receive the interest from the poor. It remains in the poor neighborhoods, being recycled over and over again. Biblical principle? I think so. Updated for the Third Millennium? Definitely.

If you happen to see your enemy's cow or donkey running loose,
take it back to him. If his donkey has fallen under its load, help him
get the donkey to its feet again; don't just walk off.

(EXODUS 23:4)

As Asian economies suffered sharp declines during the fall of 1998, I was interviewed by *Money* magazine. The publication was preparing an article about religious investment advisors who try to finance the things they believe are ethical, socially responsible, or values-based, or who strive to influence corporations to behave a little better in some areas of their businesses—an endeavor called "shareholder activism." I surprised the *Money* writer by saying that I was increasing my allocations to Asian stock markets because they had stumbled and they needed our help. I explained that I believed it was part of the biblical ethic to help them, even though many Americans still see Asians as the economic "enemy." (In reality, South Korea, where I was primarily investing, is the home of the largest Christian church in the world.)

The *Money* writer wrote that I was someone "who takes the idea of stewardship to unexpected lengths." The tone of the article indicated she thought I had just taken the financial equivalent of a long walk off a short pier. Yet helping others in economic need, whether friend or enemy, is still sound theology—and, therefore, sound economics. And while the Golden Rule of many world religions commands us only to *avoid doing harm* to our neighbors, Moses and Jesus commanded that we actually *do good,* not only to our neighbors but to our *enemies,* even to the point of loving them (Matthew 5:41–44).

The financial good news is that Asian markets, particularly in South Korea, all but doubled during 1999. Not only was that good news for Asia; it was good news for the United States, since our economy was also threatened by Asian instability. And, it was most definitely good news for my portfolio.

The bad news is that the *Money* article had ended with another religious advisor saying that he and other "values-based" conservative advisors had "declared war on corporate America." Though undoubtedly well intentioned, that advisor had obviously not grasped the paradox of the loving biblical ethic for prompting change in this world. He had adopted worldly strategies rather than love. As Martin Luther King Jr. put it: "If you want to change a person, you must love him. And he must know that you love him." It's actually that last part that is so very difficult but so very necessary.

That may be particularly true when engaged in social investing and shareholder activism. Many corporate leaders are surprisingly religious. But to put it mildly, the business schools—and the church—have not always helped them to integrate their thinking about morality and business. And each of us, in our own way, directly or indirectly, has too often put corporate leaders under intense pressure to produce increasing profits quarter after quarter. Frankly, most of us usually do not care how those profits are earned. But then we read a book of this nature, grow conscious of how we might be harming our neighbors and environment, grow angry rather than loving, and demand instant satisfaction of our new goals. In my experience, it is more spiritually and socially rewarding, at least when *initially* expressing concern about corporate behavior, if we avoid going to war and instead calmly explain that we love our neighbors and children so much that we're as concerned with their future well-being as we are with our own profits this quarter. And it would surely surprise and impress most corporate leaders if they heard that we love them as well, especially in today's cynical environment when the leaders of all professions seem to be guilty of malfeasance until proven innocent.

Do not mistreat a foreigner: you know how it feels to be a foreigner,
because you were foreigners in Egypt.
(EXODUS 23:9)

Most Americans do not have to climb very far in the family tree to discover their roots in a "foreign" nation. Yet ironically, Americans tend to be among the most nationalistic in their investing. (Even the official foreign aid we give is a lower percentage of our Gross Domestic Product than any major nation.) Pat Buchanan has even written an editorial in *The Wall Street Journal* that said:

> Work, save and invest here in the land of the free. . . . Let's replace ties with foreigners with ties among Americans. . . . If foreign regimes don't like the new U.S. policy, let them not like it. This is our land; America is our country; the U.S. is our market. . . . Who, after all, is the American economy for, if not for Americans?

Against that political argument we need to weigh this sentiment from theologian Reinhold Niebuhr: "Nationalism; One of the effective ways in which modern man escapes life's ethical problems."

Some Wall Street leaders, including John Bogle, claim that we should not invest in foreign nations because we can make more money at home by investing in our own companies doing significant business overseas. While I agree this may have been the case in the closing decades of the second millennium during our great bull market, I also believe it is a more questionable proposition as your perspective grows more eternal by studying the Bible and economic history. History is littered with nations, from Rome to Holland, from Great Britain to Japan, which once dominated the world's economy but later went into decline.

A few devout Wall Street leaders, such as our friend Sir John Templeton who is often called the dean of global investing, understand that there is more for a believer to understand about investing than simply considering where we might make the most money in the short-term. When America was a developing nation, European investors financed a significant percentage of our railroads and canals. That investment contributed greatly to the abundant life we now enjoy. Some believe we should do the same for other developing nations now that we are the richest nation on earth.

More recently, the American government borrowed considerable sums from foreign investors to finance the Cold War, which brought unprecedented freedom and prosperity to our land and the world. And the new millennium began with *The Wall Street Journal* reporting the irony that the Chinese, whose per capita income is a small fraction of Americans', were financing a very large percentage of our mortgages with their savings by buying our government agency bonds. Now that the Cold War is over, our federal debt is no longer the threat many perceived, and the real estate market has been strong, some believe the U.S. might finance now the needs of other nations.

Paradoxical as it might seem, some experts suggest that such foreign loans might be the most enriching course for us as well as for our neighbors. When Japan seemed to dominate the world economy during the late 1980s, Sir John in particular suggested it might be wise for them to invest some of their surpluses in other nations rather than bid their own stocks, bonds, and real estate up to speculative levels. With the advantage of hindsight, most Japanese might now agree. American investors learned, or should have learned, the same lesson after they drove Internet and technology stocks to what Sir John called "temporarily insane" levels as the new millennium began. Again, it is a paradoxical but basic spiritual and physical law that too much can be as impoverishing as too little. Flood and drought. Heat stroke and frost bite. Obesity and famine. Inflation and deflation. As the apostle Paul put it, the ideal seems to be "moderation in all things." As we will see again and again, the Bible wisely makes no exception for money.

For six years plant your land and gather in what it produces.
But in the seventh year let it rest, and do not harvest anything
that grows on it. The poor may eat what grows there,
and the wild animals can have what is left. Do the same
with your vineyards and your olive trees.
(EXODUS 23:10–11)

I can remember when my farming neighbors and relatives were careful to rotate their crops every few years so the land would not grow poor. With the advent of modern farming techniques, such as irrigation and fertilizing, it may not have been necessary to leave the land completely fallow each seventh year in order to keep it from depletion. But many people around the globe today would be enriched if they understood the land deserves a sabbath rest as much as people do. Yet if a religious leader suggested that we shut down industry each seventh year so that the air, waters, and wildlife might restore themselves, odds are good that he or she might be accused of worshipping nature. Moses had no such concern.

It wasn't long ago that a pastor disappointed my wife by preaching a well-intentioned stewardship sermon that Christians should give to our churches *instead* of giving to "save the whales." For many years, my animal-loving wife has not only volunteered as the head of our church's Stephen Ministry, taught Sunday school, arranged flowers, and coordinated hospitality hour, but she has also found time to volunteer at a local aquatic center that cares for sick and injured sea life.

The irony is that the church's finances would have been much stronger in the future had that religious leader been conscious that Moses had taught that God has provided enough for people, churches, and the "wild animals." I say this because it wasn't long after that sermon that we joined another church, which may be another indicator of how church growth and knowledge of biblical economic principles may be more intimately connected than most pastors now appreciate.

The media and well-intentioned activists undoubtedly sensationalize many environmental problems. But Jewish and Christian people should be the first to appreciate that "subdue the earth" means we should cultivate it and care for it rather than neglect it or destroy it. Fortunately, there are mutual funds that have an environmental consciousness. They are on my website at www.financialseminary.org.

Notice, however, that the teachings from Moses were directed at the individual Hebrew. We can no more shift all our environmental responsibilities to mutual fund managers than we can shift all our responsibilities for the poor onto government officials. Be conscious of our planet home and its many inhabitants in all your daily activities. As the saying goes, "Think globally but act locally." Not only will that consciousness enrich our grandchildren materially; it might enrich you spiritually if you better appreciate how rich creation is, as well as how interconnected and fragile all of reality is.

As modern philosopher Edward Lorenz puts chaos theory: "When a butterfly flutters its wings in one part of the world, it can eventually cause a hurricane in another."

Work six days a week, but do no work on the seventh day,
so that your slaves and the foreigners who work for you
and even your animals can rest.
(EXODUS 23:12)

Give it a rest! Perhaps Moses wouldn't have put it the way my teenage son does, but Moses certainly understood that rest is a vital part of God's plan. So did Jesus. He read this teaching of Moses and interpreted it, recognizing that the Sabbath and its rest were created for humankind, rather than humankind being created for the Sabbath. The Bible tells us that Jesus also grew quite tired and had to go away from the crowds who needed his help;

only then could he repeat the pray-work-play-rest cycle again. We are surely no stronger than Jesus was, nor do we have more important work to do. So, we too need to pray and rest on a regular basis.

That is why some of us might actually want to reconsider operating our businesses on Sunday. It's now generally assumed that people need to shop on Sunday because they are busy every other day of the week; thus, no business can maintain profitability unless it's open on Sunday. But there is at least circumstantial evidence that this assumption may not be as true as we believe.

Fortune magazine devoted its July 16, 2001 cover to a story entitled "God and Business: The Surprising Quest for Spiritual Renewal in the American Workplace." It contained an interesting story about a Mormon furniture dealer named Bill Child, who sold his stores to legendary investor Warren Buffett. The stores were always closed on Sunday so his employees could worship and rest. Buffett was skeptical that he could continue that practice and remain profitable. Child arranged a one-store experiment to put Buffett's skepticism to the test. Buffett was so impressed with the results of the experiment that he told Child that if he could do it with one more store, "You'll make a real convert out of me." (The Chick-fil-A restaurant chain has prospered more famously with the same practice.)

In essence, for approximately three millennia, the Sabbath has been a way of ending things and making them new. That is, it has been about renewal. So, it is appropriate that our brief reflection on the Sabbath brings us near the end of our study of Exodus. For the book of Exodus essentially describes the ending of a people's bondage and their tentative first steps into an abundant new life of freedom. Whether we read their story in the collective sense as a nation or in a more personal sense, it is a story about the journey out of political, economic, and spiritual bondage. It is a pilgrimage that every spiritual investor should make, particularly economically. That's why there is one more terribly important passage from Exodus we must explore.

---

*When Moses came close enough to the camp to see the bull-calf and
to see the people dancing, he became furious. . . . Aaron answered,
"Don't be angry with me; you know how determined these people are
to do evil. . . . I asked them to bring me their gold ornaments, and
those who had any took them off and gave them to me. I threw the
ornaments into the fire and out came this bull-calf!"*

(EXODUS 32:19,21,24)

Judaism has been called the most materialistic religion on earth. That is often said derisively, but it may actually be a compliment. For the Bible indicates that when wealth is managed in a godly way, it is good. (Of course, when it isn't managed in a moral framework, it becomes mammon.)

So unlike the adherents of some other religions, there's no need for us to sit permanently atop a mountain and contemplate the Divine. That is why the Hebrew Scriptures contain so many moral principles for daily living from which we can all learn. But from the very beginning, God, through Moses, made it quite clear that there's an enormous difference in using and even enjoying material wealth and worshipping it.

Yet this story in Exodus 32 reminds us that it is human nature to be impatient. And if people don't get what they want from God when they want it, they'll too often create gods for more immediate gratification.

The story also tells us that it is human nature for leaders to want to please the crowd. And even Aaron, one of the most memorable figures in religious history, was very human. He was also quick to invent a most implausible story to cover his weakness. It was almost as if he was blaming God for creating the golden bull. That's one act of wealth creation that God will never perform. Neither should we. Yet golden bulls remain quite abundant, if more subtle, in today's world. Some are even created by religious leaders—another important dimension of the biblical story.

That is why John Calvin always taught that if people don't worship the true God, they will worship other gods, such as money.

When you harvest your fields, do not cut the grain at the edges of the
fields, and do not go back to cut the heads of grain that were left.
Do not go back through your vineyard to gather the grapes that
were missed or to pick up the grapes that have fallen;
leave them for the poor and foreigners.
(LEVITICUS 19:9–10)

Modern economists would view that passage in Leviticus 19 as a most "inefficient" way to manage wealth. Most investment counselors might suggest that we maximize return on investment. Economists tell those of us who work to harvest all we can because "productivity" is the key to our future well-being. Political leaders tell us to harvest all we can so we can pay taxes, which the government can then redistribute to the poor. And charity leaders tell us to harvest what we can so we can give what we can. All such advice is quite logical and materially beneficial. But, let us consider the possibilities from a different perspective.

Moses saw from his higher perspective on the mountain that there are some spiritual problems with those approaches. First, while the Bible advocates productivity, it has never worshiped the concept or made it the highest value, as many economists seem to do today. In chapter seven, we will look more closely at Luke 10:38–42, which relates the story of Jesus' visit to Mary and Martha. Martha was running around being productive and efficient. Mary simply sat at the feet of Jesus. Martha asked Jesus to make Mary get busy. But he replied, "Mary has chosen the right thing." Jesus surely anticipated why *The Economist* cautioned in its special survey of Islam and the West that unless we reintegrate economic activity and spirituality, "the history books will record that the people of the West woke up during the twenty-first century to discover that the pursuit of efficiency is not the same as the achievement of a happy life. The West, they will say, found itself living in a superbly efficient but, in the end, aimless machine."

There are material as well as spiritual problems with worshipping efficiency. Failing to leave something for the able-bodied and perhaps less efficient poor could mean they eventually forget how to harvest for themselves. They might then develop a sense of dependency on government or charity, with all the spiritual and material poverty associated with that. But the problems don't stop there. Property owners might forget that we do not really own anything in the larger sense. We might then grow to believe that it is entirely up to us to decide how to manage "our" wealth. We might also develop a sense of independence from God, with all the various "poverties" associated with that. But developing a consciousness that we *all* have limited access to *God's* resources produces material and spiritual riches, as well as a sense of our common humanity.

As the third millennium begins, there are various ways to leave a little in the corners and on the vine. For example, an increasing number of financial intermediaries allow you to take a below market rate of return on a portion of your investments in order to achieve higher social returns. At an organizational level, some corporate leaders devote a small percentage of their revenues to providing schooling and job training for the unemployed. At first glance, that might seem harmful to profits. And it might be in the short-run. But the paradox is that in the long-run it could be far cheaper than paying taxes or giving charity to a permanent dependent class that could be working, paying taxes, and making charitable donations, too.

It might cost us a bit more to invest in a mutual fund that pays someone to make tough ethical decisions than to invest in an "efficient" index fund that invests in every corporate endeavor, including many questionable endeavors, but such a choice might enrich us in the long run—and not just financially and socially. From a more eternal perspective, those ideas might make all of us happier as we grow more hopeful about the direction of our country and world.

In this year all property that has been sold shall be restored to its original owner. So when you sell land to your fellow Israelite or buy land from him, do not deal unfairly. The price is to be set according to the number of years the land can produce crops before the next Year of Restoration. . . . Your land must not be sold on a permanent basis because you do not own it: it belongs to God, and you are like foreigners who are allowed to make use of it.

(LEVITICUS 25:13–23)

The Year of Restoration occurred once every fifty years. Those who sold or lost their land another way would get it back during the Year of Restoration. In essence, the Law of Moses guaranteed that those who had finally made it to the Promised Land would not lose in future generations what they had struggled to obtain. The law reflected the importance of as many people as possible enjoying the privileges and responsibilities of managing a small part of God's wealth.

But there are other principles in this teaching as well. Notice the sense of ethics when conducting business. The law had no problem with people buying and selling in the marketplace, but such transactions had to be done fairly, with buyer and seller alike conscious of each other's well-being. No "buyer beware" there. Because honoring God was foremost in their consciousness, Moses and the Hebrews understood other people would judge our God by the way we conduct our business dealings.

And, notice the law's clear admonition that we do not really own anything, but are simply stewards—individuals who temporarily care for what belongs to another. That is a message central to Jesus' economic teachings as well, as we will see later.

After the people of Israel left Egypt, the Lord spoke to Moses and said,
"You and Aaron are to take a census of the people of Israel."
(NUMBERS 1:2)

The book of Numbers tells us escaping political bondage is only the first step in a long journey toward the Promised Land of being economically, psychologically, and spiritually free. It also reminds us that an important first step in the journey to true freedom is to take an inventory of our assets, or to count our blessings. For as we will see in our study, it has long been human beings' plan to number the potential problems in the future, but it has been God's plan to number the blessings in our present.

It is no different today. For example, I was invited to be a guest on Robert Schuller's *Hour of Power* at a time when most Americans were troubled by how our nation's $5 trillion federal debt might impoverish our future. I turned to the audience and asked how many had ever heard the "numbering" of America's federal debt. Everyone had. I then asked how many had heard the numbering of assets. Not a single person had. I have since asked tens of thousands of Americans what number they would put on America's assets, and while many make wildly divergent guesses, no one has ever really known. This is despite the fact that our government numbers our assets each year just as it numbers our liabilities.

In other words, our minds have been totally fixated on the *negative* side of America's balance sheet and that has made us imagine a lot of fearful scenarios for the future. No one was thinking about the far greater positive side of our nation's balance sheet and seeing that those assets assured an affluent future. In fact, our assets have typically been *at least ten times greater,* and probably far more, than the debts we have owed to foreign nations. So, in the last half of the 1990s, the U.S. stock market recognized the tremendous value of those assets. Those very few investors who, like Sir John Templeton, numbered America's blessings in the early '90s and visualized a better future rather than focusing on the negatives and imagining their worst fears, took a giant step toward the spiritual and financial freedom of the Promised Land.

A similar story unfolded around Y2K. Most religious media leaders repeatedly quoted Ed Yardeni, the most pessimistic Y2K analyst on Wall Street and a man Wall Street had actually nicknamed "doom and gloom" during the early '90s, but some of us knew that many other analysts actually recognized the event could be *good* for business since millions of companies, governments, and ministries upgraded their information technologies.

Again, seeing the blessings of the present is far more enriching that imagining the worst about the future. As Thomas Merton told us when summarizing the journey to the Promised Land, "We are not perfectly free until we live in pure hope."

Moses said to the Lord, *"Here I am leading 600,000 people, and you say that you will give them enough meat for a month? Could enough cattle and sheep be killed to satisfy them? Are all the fish in the sea enough for them?" "Is there a limit to my power?" the* Lord *answered.*
(NUMBERS 11:21)

Can there possibly be enough resources for the future, particularly now that our planet has 6 billion people aboard?

It's a question that has bedeviled even the most faithful for millennia. It bedeviled Thomas Malthus, who was actually an ordained clergyman during the age when our country was declaring its independence. He famously predicted that because the world's population was growing faster than its food supply, humankind would soon starve. Two hundred years later, obesity is far more of a health problem in America than starvation is. Malthus never imagined how creative people would become in developing new agricultural methods such as fertilizers and high-yield seeds.

Questions about God's power certainly have bedeviled America during the OPEC-inspired oil shortages, the stock market crash of 1987, the federal debt buildup, the Y2K panic, and the debate over Social Security. Such questions also bedeviled the automobile industry during the early 1980s. Though only a distant memory now, many Wall Street analysts thought Japanese automobile companies threatened the very existence of the U.S. auto industry. At the height of those concerns, Robert Schuller was invited to Detroit to make his "tough times never last but tough people do" talk. In a later front-page article, *The Wall Street Journal* said his hope-filled talk sounded rather like Pollyanna. But, it eventually proved to be on the mark. By the time Dr. Schuller invited me to be a guest on his show, we talked about how the front pages were saying the auto companies didn't know what to do with their excess cash. And anyone who would have invested in the nearly bankrupt Chrysler when things looked hopeless would have been blessed manyfold during coming years.

As we entered a new millennium, most Americans had once again realized we were blessed to live in the materially richest nation the world has ever known. Yet, as anxieties over the looming recession have clearly demonstrated, you can be assured that economic fears will continue to bedevil us.

There can never be "enough" to satisfy us because as human beings, in the words of the Rolling Stones, we "can't get no satisfaction" for our material wants. As Pascal told us, there's a God-shaped vacuum in the heart of every human being that only God can fill. Anyone who has journeyed through life in our consumer- and advertising-oriented culture without God knows that the more we have, the more we think we need. Anyone who thinks a president, federal reserve chief, or CEO can produce enough material wealth to fill that vacuum will remain a disgruntled voter, investor, or employee.

The only freedom from our insatiable material desires comes from what Jesus called the water that quenches the spirit.

Moses was a humble man, more humble than anyone else on earth.
(NUMBERS 12:3)

Sir John Templeton has written a personal theology called "A Theology of Humility." Sharing the belief of Jesus, who said "the greatest in the kingdom of heaven is the one who humbles himself" (Matthew 18:4), Sir John believes that human pride—especially the religious pride which makes us the origins of good and evil—keeps us from knowing God and therefore from becoming greater people, greater ministers, and even greater investors. For, one dimension of God is economic reality. And the pride that says we know it all can keep us from knowing that reality which is so enriching to investors.

For example, during the early 1990s, many people grew convinced that America's economy was doomed. But Sir John was saying the collapse of the Berlin Wall in 1989 might prompt the twenty most prosperous years in human history. A decade later it was clear that he had seen things about the American economy and about economic history in general that could have enriched the rest of us as well. But ten years earlier, surprisingly few people had been truly interested in his hopeful perspective. Even fewer had been interested in actually committing God's resources to Sir John's sense of reality. Clearly, it takes something larger than oneself to have the faith and hope to invest one's personal resources, much less billions of dollars of other people's resources, the way Sir John did.

As a mutual fund manager, Sir John obviously had to make his own decisions. But he also prayed for the grace of Abraham and the wisdom of Solomon before making those decisions. And, he had the wisdom to surround himself with some of the brightest analysts and money managers possible. He then read research from other bright people. And he constantly read the Bible in order to get the perspectives of godly people in scriptural history. Much like Solomon, who prayed for wisdom but discovered that God also granted wealth, Sir John never prayed that his stocks would go up (as we're told Jabez would) but only that he might make wise decisions with God's wealth. And, unlike even most of the pastors I know, Sir John often says prayer is not about *talking* to God (Matthew 6:7–8) as much as it is about *listening* to God.

Interestingly, now that Sir John has sold his mutual funds company to finance greater spiritual riches for the world through his foundations, he continues to seek wise counsel. He has established a board of advisors comprised of world-class clergy, physicians, educators, scientists, and businesspeople. I am always humbled by the hearts, souls, and minds that I find around me during board meetings. Sir John always encourages each of us to share our best ideas with his foundations.

Ironically, I often leave those meetings to attend church and ministry boards where the only thing we are asked to share is money. Then I return home to talk with inexperienced investors who have little time or inclination to research investment options and who are told repeatedly by some brokerage firms, financial publications, and even cynical ministries that they shouldn't seek wise counsel but should go it alone. Most of those investors return much poorer to take a second look at the biblical ethic.

So whether investing time, talents, or treasure, spiritual investors will be enriched if we are humble enough to realize we don't know it all and need to know more—even if we earned the Rhodes scholarship while studying economics at Yale, as Sir John Templeton did.

———————————— ৶ ————————————

After exploring the land for forty days, the spies returned to Moses,
Aaron and the whole community of Israel. They reported what
they had seen. . . . "That land doesn't even produce enough to feed
the people who live there. Everyone we saw was very tall,
and we even saw giants. We felt as small as grasshoppers,
and that is how we must have looked to them."

(NUMBERS 13:32)

For four hundred years, the Hebrews had been assured that they were God's children, not grasshoppers, and that they would find freedom in the Promised Land that flowed with milk and honey, not giants. But, once they had escaped the political bondage of Egypt and crossed the desert, they couldn't cross the border into the land God had promised to give them. For, while free of political bondage, they were still in psychological bondage. Their minds still had the slave mentality that caused them to number the giant-sized problems in their futures. Though it had only taken a day for the Hebrews to achieve political freedom in making their exodus from Egypt, even the long and dusty journey through the desert had not gotten Egypt out of the Hebrews.

Note that none of the Hebrews other than the spies actually saw a giant. They simply listened to human authority figures who imagined God's promise was smaller than the giants' power. *It was actually the fearful imaginings on the part of those authority figures, not real giants, that kept the Hebrews away from the blessings that God had promised.*

One of the saddest parts of that biblical story is how ten of the twelve religious leaders who had been sent out as spies pandered to the people's fears rather than honoring God's promises. It is not much different today when religious leaders play to the worst economic fears of our culture rather than reminding us of God's promise of the abundant life. It would be enriching if all of us noticed that the story goes on to say that, of the twelve spies, only the two who had faith in God's promises made it to the Promised Land themselves.

Frankly, God's truth is not dependent on the majority vote of humans, even religious leaders. We will see this reality over and over as we progress in our study: Discerning between the promises of God and the imaginings of humans is one of the richest gifts of the Bible and the spiritual life.

---

*So then, you must never think that you have made yourselves
wealthy by your own power and strength. Remember that it is the
LORD your God who gives you the power to become rich.*
(DEUTERONOMY 8:17–18)

A prominent executive who is not known for his humility once remarked publicly that religion is for the weak-minded and that he was proud he was a self-made man. I felt rather sad that the gentleman had grown so disconnected from not only God and his fellow human beings but also perhaps from reality itself.

He had grown rich in the communications industry, which is very high-tech these days. Obviously, his success was highly dependent on thousands of technicians who made his daily broadcasts possible. He was dependent on the teachers who had trained those technicians. He was dependent on the thousands of scientists who had spent long hours in laboratories developing the technologies. He was further indebted to our nation's founders, who made our economic freedoms possible, and to the millions of soldiers, who had kept us free. The list of people who had helped him become "a self-made man" could fill this book many times over.

The saddest part, however, is that this particular gentleman is well known to struggle with manic depression. And psychologists tell us that the more isolated we are from our fellow human beings, as well as from the Reality that transcends our own small selves, the more likely we are to suffer spiritual poverty.

The irony of the rest of the story is that after the recent tech crash, which cut the gentleman's wealth to a fraction of what it had been, the media reported that he was very critical of his fellow executives whom he believed had impoverished him. The man who was "self-made" on the way up, became "other-made" on the way down.

Let us say a little prayer that all self-made men and women might humbly reconnect to larger realities without the pain this gentleman must suffer.

At the end of every seventh year, you are to cancel the debts
of those who owe you money.
(DEUTERONOMY 15:1)

Moses knew from experience how political bondage could impoverish people. The Law of Moses recognized how economic bondage could do the same. So, in contradiction to what we often hear in our religious media, while Jewish law always encouraged the borrowing and lending that could enrich people's lives, that same law also made provision to set God's people free of indebtedness every seven years.

These laws—along with balancing laws requiring the repayment of debts when possible—form the basis of our modern bankruptcy codes. Yet, we should also notice that the Law of Moses did not include a list of exemptions for this teaching. God was serious about debts being canceled, though we should note that the ancients borrowed only out of need, not for the wants and desires satisfied by most of our consumer loans. Still, God might be less concerned with the number of bankruptcies today than many modern economists and overly materialistic religious leaders are.

This teaching, as well as the teaching about the fiftieth-year Jubilee, also serves as the inspiration for many spiritual leaders to review periodically rich-government to poor-government loans and to discern whether there is a moral case to be made that the accumulated debts should be forgiven. Occasionally, rich countries actually promise to forgive such debts. Whether they really get around to it is another matter but at least our governmental leaders are aware that some of us care about such biblical principles.

If in any of the towns in the land that the Lord your God is giving
you there is a fellow Israelite in need, then do not be selfish
and refuse to help him. Instead, be generous and lend him
as much as he needs.
(DEUTERONOMY 15:7–8)

Ask an assembly of modern Christians how many have ever heard the injunction to "neither a borrower nor lender be" and two-thirds will probably raise their hands. Then ask if we should borrow to build a much-needed church, and many will reply that it is unbiblical to borrow. Yet many will also have large mortgages on their homes and will have borrowed money for businesses. Worse, some will have inadvertently financed, for example, highly leveraged casinos in Las Vegas by investing in junk bond funds. This

is how, often with the aid of well intentioned but uninformed religious leaders, capital is diverted from the "kingdom" to the "world."

Ideally, it's possible that spiritual investors might finance all kingdom-
building projects without using debt. But, does our dualistic thinking indicate that we believe our homes and businesses, even casinos, are higher
priorities than our churches and charities? If not, wouldn't we *prudently*
finance a church or nonprofit building by borrowing, say, up to one-half of
the building's value *when necessary?*

Our confusion on the subject of debt is only one example of how we have
mixed, or syncretized, more modern "values" with the biblical ethic. For "neither a borrower nor lender be" is actually Shakespeare. In subsequent verses
the book of Deuteronomy calls it "evil" not to make needed loans. On the
Mount, Jesus commanded, "When someone asks you for something, give it
to him; when someone wants to borrow something, lend it to him" (Matthew
5:42). Yet one of the largest religious denominations in our country has published a financial series that says the Bible wants lending and borrowing to
be "unusual." The key of course is that Jesus and the Law of Moses were talking about fulfilling human needs, not necessarily the wants and desires of the
American consumer. In short, the biblical ethic recommends that we make
plenty of *needed* loans but also discourages the maxing out of our credit
cards for luxury consumer items because that might deny other people access
to credit for what they truly need.

We've already discussed several ways to have our money reflect that balanced biblical ethic in our modern world. Another strategy is to deposit a
portion of your long-term bank deposits into one of the "community development banks" that serve our inner cities and poorer rural areas.

The South Shore Bank of Chicago is perhaps the best known of such
banks. It was featured in an issue of *Christianity Today* largely for making
church construction loans that many traditional banks won't make. Located
in what was a gradually deteriorating inner-city area, the bank was established with the help of religious and ethical investors. It pays competitive
interest rates and accepts federally insured deposits from all over the country. It uses those deposits primarily to make loans to inner-city residents who
want to refurbish affordable housing. This not only makes it possible for
individuals to own private homes that build wealth, but it creates jobs that
help people escape welfare, which is one of the returns on its loans that the

bank seeks. Turning government projects into private housing and welfare recipients into taxpayers obviously adds to the interest we receive from the bank, enriching us indirectly. Society is enriched. And everyone is enriched spiritually.

Interestingly, understanding what the Bible rather than Shakespeare says about debt can also enrich us directly. As I have mentioned already, during the 1990s, millions of Americans grew quite pessimistic over the federal debt despite the fact that debt was moderate relative to our national income, assets, and the debts of World War II. It was largely borrowed *from us* as private citizens by our government in order to win the Cold War. Yet, confused pessimists missed much of the great bull market. That is a perfect illustration of embracing isolated Bible verses that conform to Shakespeare, political ideologies, and modern values rather than conforming our thoughts to *all* God's thoughts and embracing the riches that flow from that wisdom. That may be why Jesus cautioned about those who "teach man-made rules as though they were my laws" (Matthew 15:9)!

———————————————— ❧ ————————————————

After you have taken possession of the land, you will decide you need
a king like all the other nations around you. . . . The king is not
to have a large number of horses for his army . . . he is not to make
himself rich with silver and gold. . . . This will keep him from
thinking that he is better than his fellow Israelites.
(DEUTERONOMY 17:14–17)

While Moses made it clear that a king was an idea of human beings rather than of God, Moses was nevertheless one of the earliest lawgivers. In essence, he helped to establish the government that human beings seem to need. Jesus respected that view and commanded us to "render unto Caesar what is Caesar's." And the apostle Paul told us, "Everyone must obey state authorities, because no authority exists without God's permission. . . . Show respect and honor for them all" (Romans 13:1–7). Yet each also realized that the government must operate within moral limits. As this teaching from Deuteronomy clearly demonstrates, those limits include the economic. In light of that insight, it is fascinating how many people believe that the best candidate for high office, or even for a church board, is someone who has made him or herself rich.

Government at all levels in America today directly controls about one-third of America's economy through taxing and spending. That is about where it has been for several decades, and it is on the lower end of the range for industrialized nations. Yet largely due to Cold War spending, or what the text in Deuteronomy called "many horses for [the king's] army," at the dawn of a new millennium, the *federal* government controls a little more than one-fifth of our economy through income taxes, social security taxes, and other vehicles. That is slightly higher than it has been during the post-WWII period.

A study of American history indicates that the federal government's role in the economy always expands during wartime and rarely returns to previous levels once the war is completed. (It really became entrenched after the Civil War.) At the beginning of the twenty-first century, our democracy—a political system in which the people are ideally the king—had finally balanced its budget, at least temporarily. Voters were called upon to elect representatives who were wise enough to decide whether to invest our surplus by paying down the federal debt, shoring up Social Security, and building a missile defense system, or by allowing the people to invest or spend it themselves by enacting a tax cut.

That decision would have been much easier had Moses defined the word "many" or if Jesus had detailed what is Caesar's. But they didn't. Instead, both simply promised that the decision-making process would be much easier if we're all a little more humble and operate in a loving spirit. But as we meditate on the word "many," we might begin by understanding that in a special report, *The Economist* noted that the United States spends approximately $300 billion annually on defense. Our allies in NATO Europe spend another $160 billion. Russia spends about $50 billion, Japan a little less than that, and China a little less than Japan. Great Britain, France, and Germany spend around $35 billion each. The nations with which America has been in conflict recently were not on the chart.

I was a Distinguished Military Graduate of my university. I respect our military. But that might be exactly why I often wonder if America's military hasn't bought enough "horses" to accomplish its mission of national defense.

When you build a new house, be sure to put a railing around
the edge of the roof. Then you will not be responsible
if someone falls off and is killed.

(DEUTERONOMY 22:8)

If our bulls make a habit of killing others, we are culpable even though we didn't kill our neighbor ourselves. If we dig a pit, leave it uncovered, and a neighbor falls into it, we are responsible for our neighbor's injuries. And according to this text, if a neighbor falls off our roof (where the Israelites often gathered in the evening to escape the heat) because we haven't made adequate provisions to protect him or her, we are responsible. That is, an individual's responsibility to be careful *does not* invalidate our social responsibility to care for our neighbors as ourselves.

Can you hear the ancient protests against this law? "Isn't my house expensive enough without adding a railing to protect someone foolish enough to go near the edge?" "Shouldn't he exercise greater personal responsibility for his own safety?" "Doesn't it make more economic sense for me to just donate to patch her up if she should fall in the future?"

Perhaps. But the Law of Moses recognized (to paraphrase Jesus) that human beings were not created for the benefit of economics; economics was created for the benefit of human beings. Nowhere in the biblical ethic can you find the modern value, "Nothing personal; it's just business." In the biblical ethic, every economic act is personal. Yet as paradoxical as it might seem to the modern mind, God thought that watching out for our neighbors as ourselves was a key to the more abundant life for us as well.

Think for a moment about the savings and loan problem of the 1980s. Many investors, myself included, thought we were getting ahead by earning above-market rates from shaky savings and loans. But then the government sent a larger tax bill to cover the costs of closing those S&Ls. In the wake of that reality, I and some others have earned market rates by putting our deposits in solid inner-city banks that created jobs for those who may have been on welfare. So, in addition to the moderate interest we earned from the bank, we received a lower tax bill—call it a social dividend!—from the government.

Consider another example. Many people invest in mutual funds that finance cigarette companies. They then give to the American Cancer Society or pay some of the higher insurance costs associated with smoking. Some invest in mutual funds that finance gambling companies and then give to ministries to fight the spread of casino gambling. The list goes on and on. Karl Marx, for all his misdirected ideas about other things, may have had a point when he referred to these kinds of examples as the internal contradictions of capitalism.

The more holistic biblical ethic seeks to take those contradictions out of our lives. When the biblical ethic is combined with capitalism, which is defined as the private ownership of wealth, the resulting economic system can enrich us materially without the social and psychological stresses of the contradictions. It enriches each of us, financially *and* socially, by asking us to be conscious of how *every* economic decision reflects love of neighbor as self.

———————————————— ✍ ————————————————

*When you walk along a path in someone else's vineyard, you may
eat all the grapes you want, but you must not carry any away
in a container. When you walk along a path in someone else's
grainfield, you may eat all the grain you can pull off with your
hands, but you must not cut any grain with a sickle.*

(DEUTERONOMY 23:24–25)

In the twelfth chapter of Matthew, we read the story of Jesus and his disciples walking in the wheat fields and plucking grain to eat. Yet, even though they did not own the fields, when they were challenged by the Pharisees, they were not charged with stealing but simply for doing "work" on the Sabbath. In other words, even the Pharisees did not perceive a law had been broken by Jesus and his disciples by eating grain that "belonged" to others. Even the Pharisees knew that everything belongs to God and that God has insisted that those in *true need* have a *limited* claim on God's resources, even when it is stewarded by another.

Yet, D. James Kennedy maintained in the September 1992 issue of *Religion and Liberty:* "What does the Bible say? The eighth commandment of the Decalogue states, 'Thou shalt not steal.' For two thousand years theologians have been saying that this is a guarantee of private property. . . . The Tenth Commandment is, 'Thou shalt not covet.' You should not covet anything that is your neighbor's. It belongs to him. You are not to steal it, nor even to covet it. Again, a guarantee of private property."

Dr. Kennedy's reading of the Bible is not unusual among Christian ministers—typically politically conservative ministers—in modern America. Again, this is due to our confusing the Greco-Roman ethic, and its neo-conservative version from John Locke, with the Judeo-Christian ethic. It was the "conservative" Romans who insisted that private property rights were an absolute. (It is most unlikely that Jesus or his disciples ever practiced this particular Jewish law in a field that belonged to a Roman.) On the other extreme, it was "liberal" Greeks, such as Plato, who argued that essentially *no one* has *any* rights to private property because the state, not God, owns all property.

The biblical ethic has significant advantages over the Greco-Roman ethics. The Roman ethic—which encouraged generous giving for monuments and such but little compassion for the poor—is obviously good for the strong and rich who own property but disadvantageous for those who don't. On the other hand, the recent history of communism has shown that when the Greek ethic prevails and no one owns property for which they feel personally responsible, they don't care for it very well. As the old saying goes, "That which is common to all is dear to none."

The biblical ethic solves both dilemmas. People are assigned their own property to "steward" for its true owner, God. But, the poor have a claim on those material resources as well. That benefits a far greater percentage of a nation's people than does the conservative Roman ethic. Notice, however, that the Law of Moses recognized that the claim of the community had to be limited to what the poor needed for survival. For humans being as we are, we might feel little incentive to care about raising grapes and grain if others could simply walk through our fields and take all they want. So the Judeo-Christian ethic has advantages over the Greek ethic as well.

That reality of human nature is why Jesus very realistically exhorted us to "love thy neighbor *as* thyself" rather than "love thy neighbor *instead of* thyself." That very practical commandment is also why critics such as Ayn Rand are so very wrong about Christianity being "altruistic" in a Pollyanna sort of way. For a limited number of followers such as Mother Teresa, the Christian *ideal* is to "sell what you have and give it to the poor," but the *commandment* for the much broader populace is simply to "love thy neighbor as thyself."

Again, neither Moses nor Jesus detailed what belongs to us as property owners and what belongs to our neighbors in need. But each had complete faith in the spirit of love.

FINANCIAL CONCEPTS
OF THE SPIRITUALLY WISE

"A person is more likely to be successful managing money if he uses spiritual principles; and the more you practice spirituality, the more you learn."

Sir John Templeton

———————————————— ᴂ ————————————————

"When that time comes, you will complain bitterly because of
your king, who you yourselves chose, but the LORD will not listen
to your complaints." The people paid no attention to Samuel,
but said "No! We want a king so that we will be like other nations,
with our own king to rule us and to lead us out to war
and to fight our battles." Samuel listened to everything they said
and then went and told it to the LORD. The LORD answered,
"Do what they want and give them a king."

(1 SAMUEL 8:18–20)

As a political science student, I learned that government does only two things at the most basic level: It regulates behavior and it redistributes wealth. What God tried to tell the people through Samuel, and every prophet thereafter, was that they could save a lot of bureaucratic overhead if they would simply behave themselves and live in charity with their neighbors. Or in the words of Jesus, for a more abundant life we simply have to love God and neighbor in all that we do.

But it is most rare for people to keep things that simple. Wanting to keep up with the Joneses, we want to be like other nations. Being materialistic humanists, we want visible men and women to lead us, rather than the invisible spirit of God. And we want those human leaders to fight our battles for us.

God has always given us the freedom to make those kinds of choices. And like the people of ancient Israel, we typically make the wrong ones. Then we complain about taxes, bureaucratic red tape, and all the other things that are wrong with government!

Interestingly, Samuel predicted that even God's chosen nation would spend about 10 percent of its annual income on government. Then they tithed a little more than 10 percent to the poor, foreigners, priests, and others. That is almost exactly what Americans pay in federal taxes and Social Security several millennia later. The only difference is that more social investment and human welfare is begrudgingly channeled through Washington than lovingly given in person or through the church these days. (To be fair, we should also note that many loans to the poor are channeled through institutions called banks, a process that typically has a similarly depersonalizing effect since we never come in contact with the recipient of the loan.)

Perhaps we might be inclined to live in a more godly way if we calculated what 10 percent of our incomes each year would amount to over our lifetimes and imagined that we might keep that figure if we lived a righteous life. Some church leaders might find that to be a most "secular" or "utilitarian" reason for turning back to God. Samuel apparently had no such concern because the costs of government are a simple reality.

---------------------------------- ∽ ----------------------------------

"O Lord, . . . give me the wisdom I need to rule your people
with justice and to know the difference between good and evil."
The Lord was pleased that Solomon had asked for this,
and so he said to him, "Because you have asked for the wisdom to
rule justly, instead of long life for yourself or riches, or the death
of your enemies, I will do what you have asked. . . .
I will also give you what you have not asked for: all your life
you will have wealth and honor."
(1 KINGS 3:7–13)

This is the paradox of spiritual investing: Seek the humanity of Abraham who preferred peace among relatives to the best grazing lands and the wisdom of Solomon rather than the riches of the world, and God *might* choose to provide the greatest of material riches as well. But, first things first.

Yet, ask most modern Christians why they invest where they do and they will reply, "To make the most money." Ask why they work where they do and they'll probably say the same. It is the same answer that non-Christians give. It is the same answer that prompted one observer to say that the essence of America is to make money, in order to make more money, in order to. . . . Well, you get the idea.

Most cultures since biblical times, religious and nonreligious, have been money oriented. After Jesus made his famous statement that we "cannot serve both God and money," the Scriptures went on to comment, "When the Pharisees heard all this, they made fun of Jesus, because they loved money" (Luke 16:14). Jesus wasn't addressing the pagan world with his admonition. He wasn't foretelling a time when modern America would need to hear the message. He was addressing the religious leaders of ancient Israel. That is why even Karl Marx cynically observed: "Money is the jealous god of Israel, beside which no other god may exist." Marx would most likely say the same about America today.

Other than knowing that people such as Marx would judge God by our attitudes toward money, why was Jesus so concerned? Paradoxically, he undoubtedly knew that being overly focused on money produced a less abundant life. Think of those who pursue quick riches in our nation's casinos and day-trading brokerage firms or by trading options and commodities. Studies say about 90 percent of them lose financially. The rest lose spiritually, suffering from stress, anxiety, and loss of purpose and meaning in life.

Even some very successful businesspeople know that getting too focused on money can be equally harmful when running businesses. For example, Robert Lutz, the former president and vice-chair of the Chrysler Corporation, wrote his book *Guts: The Seven Laws of Business That Made Chrysler the World's Hottest Car Company,* after retiring. Law #1 in his book is: "The customer isn't always right." Anyone who has ever read the biblical accounts of the activities at the base of Mount Sinai or the mob that cried "Give us Barabbas"—or who watched modern investors speculate wildly in real estate, oil, and gold in the 1980s and in Internet stocks in the '90s—realizes Lutz was on to something of biblical proportions with that law.

And Lutz's Law #2 may be more so as it states: "The primary purpose of business is not to make money." That's not a misprint. He said "*not* to make money." Lutz goes on to explain how Chrysler nearly bankrupted itself thinking money was its primary purpose. The company only turned around when it realized its true purpose was to produce the best possible cars for its customers. Paradoxically, that revised understanding made the company very profitable. But, Chrysler had to do what was right and do what was good for its neighbors, rather than serving money, in order to see those profits.

---

*The king ignored the advice of the older men and spoke harshly to
the people, as the younger men had advised. He said, "My father
placed heavy burdens on you: I will make them even heavier."*
(1 KINGS 12:13–14)

The primary economic lesson from the kings of Israel is quite simple: With spiritual maturity comes the wisdom that the lighter the burden of government, the more blessed the nation is—and perhaps the longer the reign of the king!

C. S. Lewis expounded on this sentiment in *Mere Christianity* when he wrote:

> It is easy to think the State has a lot of different objects—military, political, economic, and what not. But in a way things are much simpler than that. The State exists simply to promote and to protect the ordinary happiness of human beings in this life. A husband and wife chatting over a fire, a couple of friends having a game of darts in a pub, a man reading a book in his own room or digging in his own garden—that is what the State is there for. And unless they are helping to increase and prolong and protect such moments, all the laws, parliaments, armies, courts, police, economics, etc., are simply a waste of time.

---

*"I intend to build a great temple, because our God is greater
than any other god. Yet no one can really build a temple for God,
because even all the vastness of heaven cannot contain him.
How then can I build a temple that would be anything more
than a place to burn incense to God?"*

(2 CHRONICLES 2:5)

If you have ever visited the Crystal Cathedral or seen the *Hour of Power*, you know that millions of people have given time, talent, and treasure so that tens of millions might glimpse the glory of God. You may also appreciate that sociologists say a society's highest values are always reflected in the highest buildings in town. During the age of religion, church spires dominated the skyline. During the age of government, courthouses towered over town squares. And now that business dominates, office buildings spear the skyline.

Still, we board members of the Cathedral have always understood, as Solomon did, that our creative efforts surely pale in comparison to what God has created in our universe home. That is actually why the Cathedral is built of glass. Dr. Robert Schuller is convinced that people were intended to worship, sing, and pray in a garden-like setting. That feeling is often augmented when a few sparrows fly through the open windows of the Cathedral! Yet we also understand, as Solomon did, that we have not created a box within which we can "contain" God until we return next Sunday. It is simply a place from which our awe of God and creation can emanate to the far corners of the world.

Still, we are often criticized for spending money on the Cathedral rather than on the poor. For example, if you have read the wonderful book *Rich Christians in an Age of Hunger* by Ron Sider, you know that Dr. Sider is rather critical of the money we have spent on buildings while so many of the world's poor are hungry. I often reflect on the morality of the same, as does every member of the board and Dr. Schuller himself—who believes we would have even more poor if they didn't have jobs such as building Cathedrals! Yet, each of us also knows how we have fallen to our knees when visiting the great cathedrals of Rome and Europe. I then ask myself, "Hasn't God given us enough to both feed the poor and to pour lavish worship upon our God?"

Jesus apparently thought so. The Christian Scriptures tell us that a woman poured "expensive perfume" on Jesus only to hear the disciples critically ask, "Why all this waste? This perfume could have been sold for a large amount and the money given to the poor!" They must have been shocked when Jesus responded, "Why are you bothering this woman? It is a fine and beautiful thing that she has done for me" (Matthew 26:6–10).

In short, such thinking as the disciples' and Dr. Sider's typically reflects scarcity thinking. Jesus would have none of it because he knew God to be a God of abundance. So, before one group of Christians critique another for pouring money into cathedrals and before the second group criticizes the first for pouring money into the proverbial "rat holes" of developing countries, let's all pause and look carefully at where each of us has invested all God's resources. We may find that significant portions of what we steward in mutual, endowment and pension funds haven't honored God as *either* building cathedrals or feeding Third World countries might have done. Then, we might finally realize that God has always provided more than enough to finance God's kingdom.

He took all the survivors to Babylonia, where they served him
and his descendants as slaves until the rise of the Persian Empire.
And so what the LORD had foretold through the prophet Jeremiah
was fulfilled: "The land will lie desolate for seventy years,
to make up for the Sabbath rest that has not been observed."
(2 CHRONICLES 36:20–21)

There are few people on earth as appreciative of God's grace as I am. I am profoundly grateful that I do not always get what I deserve but rather what a gracious God has chosen to give. Yet, I also believe in a *limited* version of the law of cause and effect. For while God does many miracles in my life, as this passage in 2 Chronicles relates I daily see terrible consequences for disobedience, especially in the realm of economics.

What we saw in Exodus 23:10 was repeated in Leviticus 25:1–7: The law's requirement that the agricultural society let the land rest each seventh year. The people's disobedience seemed a more profitable approach in the short-term. But it was devastating in the long run.

It was not so different when the industrial West made the transition from an agricultural society to an industrial society. During the roaring '20s, it seemed that all limits to economic activity had been repealed. The Great Depression in the 1930s proved that they had not. The same laws seemed to have been repealed during the booming '50s. The environmental problems that contributed to the social upheaval of the late 1960s proved once again that they had not.

As we enter a new millennium, we are rapidly transitioning from an industrial society to a knowledge society. And it is now suggested that there are no limits to knowledge. It is suggested that this will necessitate a new economics for the world. There may be some truth in that, as expressed in the proverb: "If you have a dollar and I have a dollar and I give you my dollar, you have two dollars and I have none. But if you have an idea and I have an idea and I give you my idea, you have two ideas but I still have mine."

Still, as a knowledge worker who is essentially compensated for his ideas, I might suggest that the sabbath rest will be just as important to a knowledge society as it was to earlier agricultural and industrial societies. We need to take a break from exchanging ideas just as badly as we need time to take a break from exchanging grain or cars. As Solomon put it in Ecclesiastes 12:12: "Son, there is something else to watch out for. There is no end to the writing of books, and too much study will wear you out."

Or as Naomi Judd, the entertainer who has long been a friend of the Crystal Cathedral, likes to say, we need time to simply be human beings rather than human doings . . . or even human thinkings! Note a critical distinction, however: Prayer and meditation are not thinking. And that is a most significant fact for knowledge workers.

When I was very young, I found it rather simple to leave my chores behind and pray in solitude on the river in the back of our farm. When I worked my way through college, it was easy to leave my construction job behind and pray in the solitude of my car on the way home. But now that I'm a knowledge worker, it seems far more difficult to get away from my thoughts to pray and meditate. Fortunately, the extra effort is even more worth it.

———————————— ✌ ————————————

"I have let the people borrow money and grain from me, and so have
my companions and the men who work for me. Now let's give up all
our claims to repayment. Cancel all the debts they owe you—money
or grain or wine or olive oil. And give them back their fields,
vineyards, olive groves and houses right now!"

(NEHEMIAH 5:10–11)

Again, we see the principle that, contrary to what most American Christians believe and may actually have been taught, freely lending to those in need has long been a key biblical concept. What the Bible is actually skeptical of, yet what many American Christians are taught is morally correct, is the earning of interest and the insistence that borrowers have an absolute moral obligation to repay their loans.

With the advent of modern banking during the Industrial Revolution, the Protestant reformers agreed that Christians could morally earn interest on productive, as opposed to consumer, loans. Their reasoning, quite correct in my opinion, is that if I lend you money to plant your crops and you prosper, we are both ahead if you essentially share some of your harvest with me by paying me interest. However, if I lend you money to buy the food you need today, you consume it and tomorrow you have nothing with which to repay me the principal, much less any interest on that debt. So, in the cases of greatest need, the reformers maintained, I should simply give to you rather than loan to you.

But, for those whose misfortune was simply light or temporary—if, for example, your crop fails and you have nothing with which to repay my loan or interest—the reformers believed the only moral thing to do was to forgive your loan, interest and all. They called this the principle of "shared risk" in lending. As Martin Luther put it in his typically outspoken manner:

> If, after diligent work, his efforts fail, he who has borrowed money should and may say to him from whom he borrowed it: This year I owe you nothing; for although I sold you my work and labor to get you a percentage of profit on this and that property my efforts were not successful. The loss is yours and

not mine; for if you want to have a share in winning, you must also have a share in losing. The nature of every business transaction demands this. The moneylenders who do not want to put up with these terms are as pious as robbers and murderers and rob the poor of his possessions and livelihood. Woe to them!

These teachings present quite a problem for more of us in financial services than for loan officers at banks. For example, I once received several calls from a broker who had been reading my books. He was a fundamentalist Christian who was deeply stressed to think he was violating a biblical principle by helping fellow Christians earn interest by lending money or by buying bonds. I gradually helped him understand that either he had to accept that church *tradition* now allows him to do so (assuming the bonds are financing production rather than consumption), or he had to find a new vocation. I do not know what decision he ultimately made, but I admire him for struggling with the question.

Perhaps more people around our world would admire Christianity if more of us struggled with how many biblical, and even traditional, principles are in tension with even the simplest economic activities, such as investing in CDs or bonds. Sure, no one likes tension, but establishing a moral framework for our economy would surely make it creative tension.

Satan replied, "Would Job worship you if he got nothing out of it?
You have always protected him and his family and everything he
owns. You bless everything he does, and you have given him enough
cattle to fill the whole country. But now suppose you take away
everything he has—he will curse you to your face."
(JOB 1:9–10)

A well-known evangelical financial author began a book a few years back with this statement: "Suddenly, I felt the subconscious click of the proverbial light bulb: The biblical principles of money management that I had been teaching and using for years would work under any economic scenario.

Armed with these concepts, I knew exactly how to help our clients weather the coming storm, no matter how hard the financial winds blew."

That's a tremendously appealing concept, especially as the book promised shelter from an economic storm that had been widely predicted by another best-selling evangelical book. And as any retirement planner, insurance agent, and even newspaper publisher knows, either consciously or subconsciously, there's no more effective marketing technique than to frighten people and then ease their anxieties by promising you can protect them if they'll simply buy your product.

In my view, the book offered genuine help in such areas as budgeting and credit-card debt. Yet, it was also a case study in how we can quote a few Bible passages and miss the true spirit of the Bible. We then create a cultural theology reflective of the place and time, or perceptions, in which we live, and thereby help Christians see reality through a distorted cultural screen rather than a clear biblical screen. For the reality is that *the Bible, including the Jewish Scriptures, positively and absolutely has never, ever offered anyone a financial guarantee of principal.* To believe and teach that it does is to turn the ancient Scriptures into New Age entertainment, a Disneyland where everyone is healthy and wealthy.

That may be why the book of Job, and perhaps the book of James, are the least quoted by those who write financial books for American Christians. For while *selected* passages from the books of Moses and Solomon seem to offer assurances to the *community* that righteousness and wealth always go hand in hand, Job tells us that may not always be true for the *individual*. (As we will see in chapter 8, James told us we may not even *want* wealth to accompany our faith, which is one reason, along with it being a book that seems to emphasize works rather than grace, Luther referred to it as "the epistle of straw.")

Reading the Bible without our cultural screen, we can see why Job remains a book that our Christian brothers and sisters in Africa and other parts of the world deeply appreciate. Winston Churchill once described Uganda as "the pearl of Africa." At one time that beautiful land flowered with tea, coffee, and wildlife. But Idi Amin destroyed much of it. And with it, he destroyed the wealth of hundreds of thousands of faithful Christians. That scenario has been repeated since the days of Job. Both my devout father, who died very young from cancer, and the Ugandans have drawn faith from the trials of the righteous Job, who was most definitely not sheltered from the storms of life. Perhaps God will provide material riches for the Ugandans once again. Perhaps, like my father, they will find that God chooses to provide even greater riches of a spiritual nature.

Why does God let evil men live, let them grow old and prosper?
They have children and grandchildren, and live to watch them
all grow up. God does not bring disaster on their homes;
they never have to live in terror. . . . They live out their lives
in peace and quietly die without suffering.
(JOB 21:7–9, 13)

As I learned when my father lay on his deathbed, it is difficult enough to acknowledge that seemingly bad things do happen to good people. But, as I also learned in subsequent years on Wall Street, it may be even more difficult to look around and realize that seemingly *good* things happen to *bad* people. However, as Job also discovered, it is extremely difficult from our human perspective to understand exactly what the good things are and what the bad things are, and who the good people are and who the bad people are.

Job thought it was a bad thing when he lost his wealth. But would there be a book in the Bible about him had he not? He thought his wealthy friends were good people. But they disappointed him with their criticisms and temptations to curse God. Job seemed to think that good people should die without suffering. But my father, who read the book of Job over and over during the year he suffered on his deathbed, never complained about what God asked him to bear. His spiritual example is more of a blessing to me than any amount of money he could have left to me.

Even on a more "worldly" level, how many of us have thought something good had happened to us only to realize later that it wasn't so good after all? I was once disappointed that I wasn't named the manager of an E. F. Hutton office I coveted. But had I gotten that job, I may have lost my career a few years later, since the regional manager to whom I would have reported later helped bring the firm down with some shady dealings.

How many of us have been betrayed by someone we trusted, such as a favorite analyst turned wrong by human greed and pride? Who hasn't been surprised at a totally unexpected act of grace, like a bad investment bailed out by a takeover? Who hasn't had a major disappointment that eventually revealed itself as a blessing in disguise? I was once treated poorly by a manager of a Wall Street firm only to find that his unethical act—which was repeated against several brokers who worked for him—encouraged me to rearrange my business in a way that blessed me beyond measure during coming years.

As humans with a limited perspective of things, we can't always understand these things. We simply have to have faith that all things work for the good of those who love God.

The wicked man borrows and never pays back.
(PSALM 37:21)

This is the moral balance to seventh-year and Jubilee-year loan forgiveness. There *is* a moral obligation to repay what we have borrowed when possible. After all, anything we have borrowed was first put into that person's stewardship by God. If we are to honor God, we must honor that as a moral reality. Also, we might dishonor God in the eyes of the lender if we do not honor the arrangement.

That being said, however, notice that this passage simply indicates that it is wicked to "never" repay. It does not say that we're wicked if unusual circumstances make it impossible for us to repay. That is made equally clear by other passages in the Scriptures, such as the passage about seventh-year debt forgiveness.

A healthy balance of repayment when possible—and not simply convenient—but debt-forgiveness when debt is truly burdensome is what our modern bankruptcy laws and foreign policies regarding Third World debt should move toward. It is what we should strive to achieve in all our personal borrowing and lending as well.

———————————— *ഗ* ————————————

Don't put your trust in human leaders;
no human leader can save you.
(PSALM 146:3)

After the passage of a bill designed to address the budget deficits of the mid-1990s, a young leader of Congress emerged to enthusiastically declare that his party had "saved America." Several of my friends who were members of his political party, as I was, seemed to agree.

I was intrigued by the perspective. As a percentage of our economy, the federal deficit had actually peaked ten years earlier when most of my political friends didn't know what a budget deficit was. It had been declining even more rapidly after the fall of the Berlin Wall ended the higher defense spending of the Cold War. Yet the young congressman and my friends seemed more inclined to believe human leaders had saved America rather than to acknowledge that the march of God's grace and justice had continued with the fall of the Wall.

Had we been able to see events from God's much larger perspective, perhaps our nation, and Christianity in particular, wouldn't have been so deeply divided and spiritually impoverished by economic anger and anxiety during those days. So we must be careful not to see the word *leader* in a purely political perspective. They can be economic. *Time* magazine has even named Alan Greenspan the "leader of the committee to Save The World."

There are also religious leaders, particularly media celebrities within media-driven evangelicalism, in whom people place their trust to save the world, themselves, and their personal wealth as well. That can be just as impoverishing as placing your trust in political leaders as it is no less idolatry. Which is why even *Christianity Today* has editorialized: "Wisdom demands that we become suspicious of celebrities. A big, red, 'be skeptical' sign should flash in our minds whenever we see Christian personalities plastered on our book and magazine covers or hear their smooth voices sweetening our TVs and radios ... We need to recognize the painful truth that the pervasiveness of worldly entertainment values within the evangelical subculture has a tendency to minimize the gospel content."

———————————— ✍ ————————————

Getting wisdom is the most important thing you can do.
Whatever else you get, get insight. . . . Nothing will stand in your
way if you walk wisely, and you will not stumble when you run.
Always remember what you have learned.
Your education is your life—guard it well.
(PROVERBS 4:7, 12–13)

During the mid-1990s, millions of Americans were very anxious about the federal debt. Virtually everyone could share with me the *information* that we had a $5 trillion debt. But when I asked who knew to whom we owed that debt, few could tell me. And when I asked how that debt related to our assets, no one knew. The very few true economists who knew those things had a deeper understanding, or wisdom, and did not typically see the debt as that significant in the scope of things. As a result, they were far more likely to be at peace and participate in the strong economy and bull market of the '90s.

Similarly, Focus on the Family broadcast a panel discussion about the computer problems many had predicted for January 1, 2000, which were known as Y2K. Of the half-dozen panelists who participated in the discussion, only one actually worked in the computer industry. The rest seemed simply to be selling books about Y2K. As *The Wall Street Journal* noted in a front-page feature article soon after the panel discussion, the computer expert was by far the most hopeful about Y2K, although even he was less optimistic than many other computer experts were.

As wise old Solomon tried to tell us in Proverbs 4, there is enormous difference between "information," which is wide and shallow in our politically obsessed and media-dominated culture, and the far more rare "wisdom" and "insight" that enrich life, first spiritually and then, perhaps, financially.

That's why Nobel-Prize-winning economist Douglas North has formulated a concept he called "asymmetric information." He essentially maintained that most people make financial decisions out of the information that is aggressively marketed to them each day. But a few people, what we might call the "smart money," make their decisions out of the insight and wisdom they work hard to find for themselves.

In our far more complicated culture, none of us can be an educated expert in the dynamics of the federal budget, computer programming, and all the various issues that concern Americans each day, including investment planning. That is why other passages in the Bible suggest we should be humble enough to listen to those who are wiser than we are in aspects of life that are outside our areas of expertise.

Also, remember that Proverbs 17:16 realistically balances the previous passage with: "It does a fool no good to spend money on an education, because he has no common sense." As much as it pains this board member of a Christian college to counsel, foolishly spending money even on education is not wise stewardship.

Lazy people should learn a lesson from the way ants live.
They have no leader, chief or ruler, but they store up their food
during the summer, getting ready for winter.
(PROVERBS 6:6–8)

From a balanced biblical perspective, there is far more to work than simply earning a living by the sweat of our brow. There is something *natural* about it. It is not something a boss should demand from us each day on the job. It is not something a political leader should require or encourage from us through fiscal policies. It is simply something that we were created to do. Working is an integral part of the abundant life, as many of the retirees I have counseled over the years have discovered.

On the other hand, there are several other biblical passages that caution against working too hard, building "bigger barns" that help us to hoard our excess and "storing up treasures on earth" rather in heaven. And while this passage in Proverbs 6 is popular with Christian financial authors who advocate the more material approach to life, Jesus actually asked us to observe the lilies of the field who "spin not" but are still cared for and are most beautiful.

Read in isolation, any of these passages can proof-text an extreme approach to life in either direction. But read as an integral part of the whole, they indicate the biblical ethic regarding work and saving is one of healthy material and spiritual balance.

Being lazy will make you poor, but hard work will make you rich.
(PROVERBS 10:4)

It is the LORD's blessing that makes you wealthy.
Hard work can make you no richer.
(PROVERBS 10:22)

The apparent contradiction in these two proverbs brings us to a time for a bit of deeper, more nuanced theology. Over the years, I've worked with several conservative religious groups. I've occasionally been asked to sign a statement of faith that indicates I believe in the "infallibility" of Scripture. Essentially, that indicates I believe everything necessary for salvation can be found in the Bible. Having grown up with a conservative view of Scripture, I'm always happy to do so.

But on other occasions, I've been asked by very conservative groups to sign a statement that I believe in the "inerrancy" of Scripture. I've always been reluctant to do that. It's not that I don't believe in inerrancy. It's just that I'm not formally trained theologically, and passages similar to those above seem to me to be in conflict. That doesn't mean they *are* in conflict. It just means that my limited human perspective cannot allow me to see, for example, how hard work can both make us richer and not make us richer. So, I can't sign a statement of inerrancy with integrity until I better understand. To add to my hesitancy, Dr. R. C. Sproul has explained in *Grace Unknown* that Protestant theologians often say that the doctrine of "inerrancy" applies to the *original* manuscripts, which we do not have access to, rather than to today's translations. How am I to know if the original manuscripts were inerrant if we don't have access to them? Yes, I know . . . by faith. Call me a doubting Thomas but integrity demands that I reserve my faith for God until I better understand what I can see. At the very least, if everyone adopted that skepticism, we wouldn't have as many biblically ignorant people claiming that their questionable worldviews are absolutely biblically inerrant.

Yet, I will venture an opinion as to how even my limited understanding can reconcile these particular passages. Financially speaking, I was most fortunate to be born in America. When I was young, my father showed me that hard work did indeed lead to greater material wealth. I've discovered the same during my career. So the first passage does indeed seem correct culturally. Yet several years ago, I was invited to speak in Uganda just after Idi Amin had destroyed that once beautiful country. The average Ugandan made about $1 per day. Some of them worked far harder than I did in my Wall Street office. Yet they were hardly growing rich from their labor. So, the second passage also seems true. It simply acknowledges that there are cultural contexts in which both are true.

Whether my opinion accurately resolves the seeming conflict in the passages or not, there are two lessons in this passage. First, it is easy to find an isolated verse that serves our own needs. If I am a bit hyper and preoccupied with making money, I might prefer the first verse. If I am more laid back, however, I might prefer the second verse. Second, reflecting on our personal *experiences* as well as on church tradition and our own reasoning can complement the literal reading of Scriptures in helping us to a fuller understanding of reality. While Jesus certainly read and appreciated the ancient Scriptures, even he told us to observe the birds of the air to learn about life in God's world. We should simply anchor our traditions, reasoning, and experiences firmly in the Scriptures, as Jesus did.

Don't build your house and establish a home until your fields are ready, and you are sure that you can earn a living.
(PROVERBS 24:27)

Sir John Templeton was a young man during the Great Depression. He and his young bride furnished their first apartment for $25 by going to garage sales. That allowed them to save fifty cents of every dollar they earned. While both choices would seem most strange to young people today and would horrify most merchants, the Templetons decided they would make it fun.

And as a result of those choices, John was able to take advantage of opportunities as they came along over the decades.

My wife and I did not go that far, but we have practiced much the same philosophy. While we did not grow up during an economic depression, we both grew up relatively poor. We married and moved to Florida without enough to pay a month's rent. Since it was summer in Florida, we found a complex that was offering a month's free rent for a year's lease. We used two large logs for coffee tables and a few bricks and boards for a bookshelf. Over the next two decades, we never lived in a house whose total value exceeded our annual income, although our bankers and real estate agents always quoted the conventional wisdom that we could afford a home whose mortgage alone was two and one-half times our annual income. But we were able to save 25 percent of our earnings during those years.

We are very aware how incredibly blessed we were to be in the securities business during the greatest bull market in history. And we know that from a purely financial perspective, we may have been better off to leverage up as housing has appreciated. But even today, fellow investment advisors who also worked during that bull market ask how my wife was able to quit full-time employment when our son was born and how I can afford to write books and serve on all the boards that I do. The simple answer is implicit in the proverb above. It is called "delayed gratification."

Sociologists have conducted studies with children that show kids who can wait a few minutes for two cookies rather than eat one now are far more likely to achieve financial stability in life. Frankly, my teenage son doesn't always like that concept any more than most of my clients do. But he is learning to appreciate it. He gets an allowance for doing certain chores around the house that are a bit beyond his normal contributions. After tithing, he gets to make the decision about whether to spend his money, put it safely in the bank, or risk it in a mutual fund. He can use that money anytime he chooses. While he is often tempted to use it a bit foolishly, the important point is that he has regularly had to decide whether to buy a cheap something now or a better something with each passing week, month, or year.

I hope that you will find your own way of teaching your children this basic but enriching biblical concept.

When a nation sins, it will have one ruler after another.
(PROVERBS 28:2)

Kennedy, Johnson, Nixon, and Ford. . . . Vietnam, Kent State, Birmingham, and Watergate. . . . I studied political science during the late 1960s and early '70s. Those years were a period of moral turbulence. They were also a period of skepticism, even cynicism, toward our national leaders and government in general. In some ways, those sentiments remain with many of my fellow baby boomers today.

Yet this verse in Proverbs 28 might suggest that we give government a break. Notice it does not say, "When a nation has one ruler after another, it sins." The verse says the problem begins with the moral condition of the people. Although people who are in spiritual turmoil will always find it convenient to project that turmoil onto their leaders, even conservative political philosopher Edmund Burke agreed that this passage had it correct. He said, "A mean, corrupt, careless, sluggish people will never have a good government of any kind."

Or, as C. S. Lewis put it: "A sick society must think much about politics, as a sick man must think much about his digestion."

We will see in subsequent chapters, however, that other biblical passages indicate the moral condition of a nation's leaders often trickles down to the populace, rather than the other way around, as this passage indicates. But, when you are tempted to focus politically on Washington in order to cure what ails our culture, *first* take a spiritual look within. If that seems in good order, *then* take a look around at the spiritual condition of your neighbors. You may not have to look as far away as you expected.

If you are in a hurry to get rich, you are going to be punished.
(PROVERBS 28:20)

As the new millennium dawned, the Nasdaq was making a remarkably irra-tional run to the five thousand level. John Templeton called it the greatest financial bubble in the history of the world. And *The New York Times* quipped, "It is not just getting rich but getting rich fast that's the new religion."

At that time, I met church leaders who spent every day sitting in day-trad-ing brokerage offices. I met others who were at home trading online. One church treasurer told me that it didn't matter that Nasdaq companies had no products, earnings, or prospect of earnings; the only thing that mattered was that their stocks were going up and you could make money by trading them.

But as the subsequent crash proved, the new religion was a false one. And most converts to it were eventually punished. Most were punished finan-cially as studies indicate more than 90 percent of those traders lost money. Yet even those who prospered financially may have been spiritually harmed. Trading involves enormous stress. It surely distracts us from activities that are more beneficial to our neighbors, which are a surer road to our own riches. And it probably can't build strong character to believe that you can make money without helping other people.

Yet many of the rest of us *unwittingly* engage in such activities. During the 1990s, even the *typical* mutual fund manager traded all our stocks about every year. Some of the most popular mutual funds traded them every three to four months. The Vanguard mutual funds—which admittedly have a vested interest in convincing us to put our money in a passive index fund and forgetting about it—has published a study that showed a very direct link between excessive trading and low returns, even before taxes were factored in.

As if that trading by our fund managers wasn't enough, the typical mutual fund investor has been trading his or her own mutual fund every two years. Yet studies also show that you could actually *add one-third to your returns by investing when others are selling their funds*. After twenty years in this busi-ness, I make many of my personal investments by doing the *opposite* of what services tell me most investors are doing. The majority of my friends in the business who have the most experience and wisdom do the same thing.

If you truly understand how markets work, you know that approach to be valid. Because the only thing that moves a market is supply and demand, the prices of assets always bottom at the point of lowest demand and always peak at the point of highest demand. The difficult trick is to know how to discern "lowest demand" from "highest demand"! If you are to buy low and sell high, you simply have to do the opposite of what most people are doing.

Such insights notwithstanding, I have grown to believe that the greatest losses related to speculation are most probably in the spiritual realm, even for those who prosper financially. I was once invited to a major radio station for a debate over the federal debt. A gentleman, who was a serious Christian who had made a fortune by trading commodities on the floor of the Exchange, railed that the debt was pushing America over a financial Niagara Falls. As the debate went on, I realized he was basically overly sensitive to our government engaging in any form of leverage, or borrowing, because he himself lived in the most leveraged sector of our economy and daily saw the damage done by, in his words, "borrowing and speculating."

Because our government had been borrowing money to win the Cold War rather than to speculate, his perspective was another simple case of seeing things not as they are, but as we are. And, fundamentally, despite having grown financially wealthy in his get-rich-quick world—which is a get-poor-quick world for about 90 percent of the people who visit it—he was in deep spiritual poverty. And he was most definitely being punished, despite his financial "success."

Show me a righteous ruler and I will show you a happy people.
Show me a wicked ruler and I will show you a miserable people. . . .
When the king is concerned with justice, the nation will be strong,
but when he is only concerned with money, he will ruin his country.
(PROVERBS 29:2, 4)

A few pages back, we read that an immoral people will never have moral government. Now we read that morality and spirituality start at the top.

The recent experiences of Americans may validate both. "It's the economy, stupid," was a campaign theme that moved the relatively unknown governor of Arkansas into the most powerful office in the world. It resonated with a highly materialistic electorate. But that leader's sexual immorality made the people "miserable" and almost moved him out during impeachment hearings.

I later talked with one of the three pastors I know who had had President Clinton's ear. He said the president had asked him what one thing he could do to put the country on the right track. The pastor had replied, "Pay off the federal debt." I told the pastor that there were a couple things I might have suggested to the president that might have made the electorate far happier. The point is simply this: Particularly in our democracy, in contrast with the theocracy of biblical days, a nation tends to get the leadership it wants and deserves. If we are focused on money rather than morality, we will get a president who is focused on money rather than morality.

If the Bible is in touch with reality, and I believe it still is, focusing on money will only ruin a democracy, perhaps financially but certainly spiritually.

I ask you, God, to let me have two things before I die: keep me from lying and let me be neither rich nor poor. So give me only as much food as I need. If I have more, I might say that I do not need you. But if I am poor, I might steal and bring disgrace on my God.
(PROVERBS 30:7–9)

The apostle Paul once summarized the Judeo-Christian ethic as the pursuit of "moderation in all things" mundane, which obviously allows us to be extreme in our love of God and neighbor. This proverb is a perfect example of that balanced ethic.

While having an excess of wealth may have some material advantages, it also has its spiritual challenges. I often meet people who seem to have grown independent of God, with all the dangers of pride and nihilism that entails. Others have grown "financially independent" of their fellow human beings, with all the problems of loneliness and other ills that entails. Henri Nouwen summarizes this ethic in his wonderful book *Lifesigns*, which claims that humankind's true needs are for intimacy, fruitfulness, and ecstasy rather than for enough money to be independent:

Those who have entered deeply into their hearts and found their intimate home where they encounter their Lord, come to the mysterious discovery that solidarity is the other side of intimacy. They come to the awareness that the intimacy of God's house excludes no one and includes everyone. They start to see that the home they have found in their innermost being is as wide as the whole of humanity.

I often meet people who are tremendously anxious about losing the wealth they have accumulated. It is as if they have no proverbial house to go to in their loneliness. And since the stock market dropped from its peak at the turn of the millennium, I have met many still-rich people who seem quite sad indeed that they were once quite richer.

Both might truly be enriched to ponder what good it does them to gain the whole world but lose their souls.

This is all that I have learned: God made us plain and simple but we have made ourselves very complicated.
(ECCLESIASTES 7:29)

Several years ago, while researching the first book I wrote about Sir John Templeton, virtually every one of his closest associates told me that the key to his great financial, and perhaps personal, success was simplicity. After studying the man for nearly fifteen years now, I believe more than ever that is true.

Sir John has one surprisingly small residence and no vacation homes. He has no yachts, airplanes, or other adult toys. When he travels, he rarely even wants us to pick him up. He usually says it will be simpler if he just grabs a cab. He has gone to the same office for several decades now. I've often seen him making his own photocopies even though he could easily afford an assistant to attend to such details. He once hand-wrote a check to me for $10 and mailed it to me after he had misunderstood a request I had made of him. He thought my request might cost me $10 and he didn't want me out that money, despite the fact he has enriched my life immeasurably over the years. That check is now on my son's bookshelf as a valued keepsake.

More importantly for investors, Sir John allows me to share that the constitution of his foundation has a very, very simple investment plan for us to follow once he has died. We are to put the funds into about a half-dozen general-purpose mutual and hedge funds and remove the poorest performing every few years. That's it. Yet Sir John believes it is the best way for future advisors, which include some of the finest investment minds in the world, to manage what will probably be hundreds of millions of dollars.

That is no late-life conviction. Sir John was famous for decades for saying most people would be better off simply to put their money in "three or four globally diversified funds that can invest without restriction in any security of any nation," such as the Templeton Growth Fund, that are "managed by the wisest possible manager" and then trust him or her to do a better job than we or our local brokers might do.

That requires a bit of humility on the part of investors and their advisors. But I have very little evidence of any philosophy that has worked better during my decades on Wall Street. As my dad used to counsel about deal making on Main Street: "If a deal can't be explained on the back of a napkin, don't do it." Sure, in our litigious society dealing on Wall Street, those people offering investments are going to have attorneys who make things quite complicated. But that doesn't mean the concept can't be simple and be explained simply.

None of us know what is going to happen,
and there is no one to tell us.
(ECCLESIASTES 8:7)

During the early 1980s, this young stockbroker listened attentively as would-be prophets projected that inflation and energy shortages would decimate the American economy. During the early 1990s, this more experienced investment advisor paid little attention when would-be prophets connected Desert Storm with Armageddon and projected that federal budget deficits would shake the American economy. By the late '90s, this far more experienced spiritual advisor realized it was quite unlikely that the God of the universe was interested in speaking to humankind about how computer programmers had created a problem that would create Armageddon-like chaos—especially precisely at the turn of the millennium as millions held their breath rather than at a time that even the Son of Man didn't know.

My early lessons were expensive. Unfortunately, they cost my early clients dearly, both spiritually and financially. The cost to me was quite high as well; I lost some clients, and some friends. We would all have been richer had I understood that when would-be prophets address the concerns of people rather than the concerns of God, they are expressing opinions rather than declaring prophecies.

There's a popular saying that good judgment is the result of experience, but experience is the result of bad judgment. Being human, we seem to learn only the hard way. But better by far than learning from our own mistakes is to learn from the bad judgment and resulting experiences of Solomon and others who made similar errors over the past four millennia.

Fortunately, not being able to see the future is no hindrance to the abundant life as it is built on faith. In *Lifesigns*, Henri Nouwen wrote: "When we are no longer dominated by fear and have experienced the first love of God, we no longer need to know from moment to moment what is going to happen. We can trust that good things will happen if we are rooted in that love."

---------------------------------- ✍ ----------------------------------

*Whenever I tried to become wise and learn what goes on
in the world, I realized that you could stay awake night and day
and never be able to understand what God is doing.
However hard you try, you will never find out.
Wise men may claim to know, but they don't.*
(ECCLESIASTES 8:16–17)

Sir John Templeton likes to say he has met two kinds of economic forecasters during his sixty years of managing money. The first type is the person who doesn't know what is going to happen. The second type is the person who doesn't know that he or she doesn't know.

Sir John never forgets to remind the board of his foundation, both verbally and in his many writings: "How little we know. How eager we are to learn."

Solomon was also no fool. So he knew what he didn't know. And he knew that God, the universe, our lives, and people are so very complex that no human mind can comprehend it all.

Today, about the only thing experienced investors know for sure is that when everyone—including the top economists but particularly journalists and broadcasters, both secular and religious—expects that something is going to happen, you can be quite confident that good money will be made by expecting the exact opposite to happen.

Those moments of near consensus are actually quite rare in the market-place. There must be some differences of opinion in order for buys and sells to take place each day. But once or twice in a decade, you may find the vast majority convinced of the same forecast. About once a lifetime, you may find nearly everyone convinced of it. It is the ability to discern those moments, but particularly the courage to act in an opposite manner, that separates the great investors from the mediocre ones.

Acting during those moments is much easier when you realize people have overestimated their ability to know such things since the days of Solomon at least.

Invest your money in foreign trade, and one of these days you will make a profit. Put your investments in several places— many places even—because you never know what kind of bad luck you are going to have in this world.
(ECCLESIASTES 11:1–2)

There's an old joke that Jesus may save, but Moses invests. Crude as it may be, there's an important element of truth in that adage. For truth be told, Jesus just wasn't all that interested in teaching us how to invest for our future material well-being. I have never believed that was because Jesus thought it was wrong or that we wouldn't have to do it. I just think he understood human nature and assumed most of us would always be quite interested enough in creating material wealth. So he focused on teaching the spiritual foundations upon which we could build a more abundant life, rightly understood. In contrast, the wisdom literature of Jesus' ancestors, often attributed to the wise and wealthy Solomon, addressed material wealth creation very directly. And there is a lot of wisdom in this short passage in Ecclesiastes 11.

First, it says to invest rather than to save. Essentially, saving is safely setting aside some resources that we expect to consume within a relatively short time. Investing is risking some of what we might consume in order to create more for the long-term. In agricultural times, saving was storing some seed to eat. Investing was putting seed in the ground. In our times, saving is putting money into a checking or savings account. Investing is putting money into, for example, an equity or stock mutual fund. While several passages encourage saving, this passage acknowledges the importance of investing.

Second, the text says to invest in foreign trade. The nation of Israel has never been blessed with abundant natural resources. In the days of Solomon, Israel was a bit like modern Japan: Though it was the center of many trade routes, it had to look abroad for many of the things it needed. If trade was conducted prudently, it not only provided what the people needed to build, such as temples and homes; it also added to the nation's wealth.

Third, the passage says you will make a profit "one of these days." Solomon was no day trader. He realized the more eternal perspective required of investors who are interested in true wealth creation as opposed to traders who are simply interested in wealth redistribution (which most ancient philosophers, and some modern ones as well, considered to be parasitic in nature).

Fourth, while the author had probably never heard our modern term *diversification*, he understood its merits. The more recent proverb says that those *saving* eggs should never put them in one basket. But it's even more important for those assuming the risks of *investing* in chickens to diversify among several hens!

Finally, we again hear that no one knows what is going to happen in this old world. So, if you are going to listen to prophets who are forecasting the future, you might want to be sure they are talking about storing up treasure in heaven. In this world, the reality is that you should diversify in some manner beneficial to your neighbors and be patient.

———————————————— ✍ ————————————————

If you wait until the wind and the weather are just right,
you will never plant anything and never harvest anything.
(ECCLESIASTES 11:4)

For almost twenty-five years, about once a day, I have heard a client or potential client remark: "Let's wait until this problem with (fill in the blank) clears
up and I'll invest then."

They don't realize that this old world will never run out of problems for
that blank. And should it seem the world has run out of problems to worry
about, it would be the *absolutely worst* time to invest. For, if the thinking that
this world can be a utopia has kept people from investing for millennia, then
the thinking that we've entered yet another "new era" of uninterrupted prosperity has made them invest at all the wrong time for just as long. "It's different this time" is the phrase Sir John has famously termed "the four most
costly words in history."

There's an old Wall Street saying that a bull market has to "climb a wall of
worry." For example, when the Dow Jones Industrial Average was under the
1000 level during the early 1980s, the vast majority of potential investors were
worried about 20 percent inflation. A little later, they worried about the
world running out of oil. Then they worried about recession, Desert Storm,
budget deficits, and Y2K.

Many Christians in particular fearfully anticipated an "economic earthquake" and failed to plant. They didn't realize that earthquakes are a natural, and probably necessary, part of God's plan. Others worried about a
hurricane-like storm. They didn't realize that South Florida prays for such
storms when the Everglades run low on fresh water and that scientists say
such storms over our oceans stir up plankton that larger sea life live on.

And, by the late 1990s the Dow had climbed beyond the 11,000 level despite
the worries.

But, by the time the new millennium had dawned, most people were convinced that we had entered the new era when technology (our latest golden
bull?) would lead us not only into a Promised Land with manageable giants,
or challenges, but a utopia with Lilliputian-sized problems. Money poured

into Internet and technology stocks and mutual funds heavily invested in both. But two years later, people had only harvested a bitter dose of short-term capital losses.

If the biblical concept of reality is correct, and I believe it is, it will be so until the end of time. Absent a major spiritual reawakening, there is little that you can do about humanity cycling between fear and greed. But there's no reason to harm our stewardship by getting caught up in the cultural drift.

Your lips cover me with kisses; your love is better than wine.
There is a fragrance about you; the sound of your name recounts it.
No woman could keep from loving you. Take me away with you,
and we'll run away; be my king and take me to your room.
We will be happy together, drink deep, and lose ourselves in love.

(SONG OF SONGS 1:14)

This may seem a strange passage to include in a book about finances, but the area of human sexuality is perhaps the one area of life other than money that people are most interested in. And the church ignores it almost as religiously as it ignores money. In fact, in my seminars, I often quip that the modern church has done to money what the Victorian church did to sex. That is, the church ignores it, so *Playboy* fills the vacuum. But I strongly believe that human sexuality is one area where the Bible has a stronger grasp of reality than *Playboy* and even the other major religions. We should therefore *invest some* of our time exploring what it says about the topic.

I like to read books from other religions. While some consider that dangerous, and it may be for immature believers who may unwittingly mix worldviews, I am never more convinced of the truth of my faith than when it is tested by other claims to truth. That is one reason I treasure a closing perspective of Ecclesiastes that says: "But because the Philosopher was wise, he kept on teaching the people what he knew. He studied proverbs and honestly tested their truth" (Ecclesiastes 12:9).

I therefore read most of the books of the Dalai Lama, who is increasingly influencing modern Americans, particularly business professionals. And as much as I admire some of his writings, such as many of those found in *The Good Heart,* in which he commented on the teachings of Jesus, it often seems his Holiness would blush at the sexual mores of the strictest Puritan! The Song of Songs has a different perspective. In short, taken literally, it seems to commend our devoting some time to a truly loving and passionate relationship with a spouse.

Sure, Jewish theologians often interpret this passage metaphorically. They believe it is about the relationship between God and Israel. Christian theologians often interpret it as the relationship between God and the church. But I'm not sure this is one area where most theologians are any more trustworthy than they are in the area of money. So, as for me and my house, we'll take Luther's advice and treat the text more literally. If the soul is about essence, or personhood, and we have been made as the Bible indicates we were, there is much more to living the abundant life in the image of God than simply being financial stewards. We must be lovers, in all the best senses of the word.

THE PASSIONATE INTROSPECTION
OF PROPHETS

"Time and again, I hear the raised voices of our would-be prophets, claiming that the cause of all our troubles is "them." . . . What we really need right now is a voice akin to the Hebrew prophets who will call us to look for the demonic within ourselves."

The Rev. Dr. Tony Campolo

ↈ

With his great power the LORD warned me not to follow
the road which the people were following. He said:
"Do not join in the schemes of the people and do not be afraid
of the things that they fear. Remember that I, the LORD Almighty,
am holy: I am the only one you must fear."

(ISAIAH 8:11)

D URING THE PAST TWO DECADES, I learned a great deal about that passage in Isaiah 8 from Sir John Templeton. When most Americans were afraid of inflation during the early 1980s, he fearlessly forecast that our stock market would triple during the coming decade.

Most Americans were fearful that Japan would buy America during the late '80s. But Sir John made what may have been his greatest calculation ever when he said the odds were quite good that the Japanese stock market would fall from the 40,000 level and the American market would rise from the 3000 level until they crossed. That happened in early 2002, near the 10,000 level.

When most Americans were afraid of recession and federal debt during the early 1990s, Sir John fearlessly forecast that we were headed for unprecedented prosperity and a soaring stock market. But when most Americans were afraid they would miss a "new economy" and the profits of soaring Internet stocks during early 2000, Sir John fearlessly forecast that 90 percent of Internet companies would soon be bankrupt and the stocks would fall precipitously.

Those predictions were always presented as calculations of probabilities and not as biblical prophecies. But indicating that the pursuit of truth is no more a democratic activity today than it was during Isaiah's time, those predictions were largely scoffed at by the public. For, while books predicting the opposite became bestsellers, Sir John had so much difficulty getting his views published that he had to establish his own printing company at his foundation. Other publishers wanted him to dilute what he truly believed with the more popular things that people feared.

I for one am grateful that Sir John was blessed with the resources to share his views, unpopular though they may have been, for they enriched my life along with those few of my clients and readers who took his unpopular views seriously. (I am also grateful that he approved the publication of this book because it had raised objections from several religious publishers, presumably since it questions much that we've gotten from religious publishers during recent years.)

If you wander off the road to the right or the left, you will hear his voice behind you saying, "Here is the road. Follow it."
(ISAIAH 30:21)

During the early 1990s, I wrote a column for a Christian financial newsletter. During my first year, despite my offering some rather enriching perspective for the readers, the publisher decided to discontinue my column.

Perhaps because I had majored in political science rather than economics in college, I could see quite clearly that the primary reason an obviously enriching relationship between Christian brothers had to come to an end was that the publisher had wandered "off the road to the right." But due to my belief in Romans 13, which was written to a group of Christians living under the barbarous Nero at the time, I could not be as angry with our own democratically elected American government as the publisher always seemed to be.

As *The Wall Street Journal* pointed out at the time, most of the angry people who dominated conservative politics at the time were not actually conservatives, safely on the right side of the road seeking limited government. They were libertarians who were angrily caught in the roadside ditch (on the *far* right) demanding a temporary shutdown or permanent elimination of government. Pat Robertson even wrote in *The New Millennium*, "The aim of free people everywhere is to limit the power and the scope of government in any way they can." The words "any way they can" struck even this conservative as extreme. We can only imagine how they may have affected more unbalanced thinkers.

Such views are always going to challenge balanced thinking and the best of relationships. Perhaps that's why our loving God has counseled moderation in all things. That's not to declare that God is a political moderate, for I hope we're seeing that God transcends all our thinking and labels. However, it may mean that some should be conservatives driving moderately on the right side of the road while liberals drive moderately on the left side of the road. It would *surely* mean that we should not worship government in the roadside ditch on the far left or hate government in the ditch on the far right. Both will surely slow our progress to the Promised Land.

———————————————— ✺ ————————————————

Is anyone more blind than my servant, more deaf than
the messenger I send? Israel, you have seen so much, but what
has it really meant to you? You have ears to hear with,
but what have you really heard?
(ISAIAH 42:19–20)

If there was one mistake that cost some of my clients more dearly than any other during the past two decades, it was believing that the opinions of would-be prophets concerning very mundane subjects could be taken as gospel.

As explained by Stephen Arterburn in *Toxic Faith*:

> Ministers, whether in a church speaking to fifty or on television reaching out to millions, are real people with real problems. They are not superhuman, and they are not immune to all the temptations of the rest of us. Even those ministers who remain faithful must be seen as imperfect and flawed. No matter how full of integrity, they cannot be the ultimate authority on every area of life. . . . When a defective pastor crops up occasionally, those who have placed their faith in him or her rather than God come to believe that God is defective. They attribute all the negative of that one individual to all people of faith. This toxic leap is irrational and is the reason many people have turned from God.

Generally, those clients who did believe in ministers rather than God were cynical toward Wall Street analysts and "secular" financial advisors because they were told often in the religious media and by religious financial books that the only "Christian" advice was "from God." Yet, *God* has told us *all too clearly* that religious pride can blind his messengers so very badly that what we hear from them is far more wrong than what we hear from avowed secularists.

Moral: For the truly abundant life, be careful to treat only the teachings of God, not those of people, even religious people, as gospel. Seek the counsel of wise persons, including religious persons. But treat it as counsel, not gospel.

I make fools of fortunetellers and frustrate the predictions
of astrologers. The words of the wise I refute and show
that their wisdom is foolishness.
(ISAIAH 44:25)

If you read *The Wall Street Journal* on a regular basis, you know that economists end each year doing two things: Making a prediction of interest rates and the stock market for the coming year, and explaining why their predictions from last year did not work out as planned.

Yet, every stockbroker and financial planner in the country also knows that if he or she doesn't provide some kind of prediction with each investment recommendation, there is little likelihood that clients will act on it.

It cannot be said often enough: Investors and their advisors, including religious authors and commentators, *cannot* see the future. But we *can* more clearly see the current needs of our neighbors and how we might meet them. That is surely a more reliable path to true riches than guessing an unknowable future.

"The kind of fasting I want is this: Remove the chains of oppression
and the yoke of injustice, and let the oppressed go free.
Share your food with the hungry and open your homes
to the homeless poor. Give clothes to those who have nothing to wear,
and do not refuse to help your own relatives.
Then my favor will shine on you like the morning sun."
(ISAIAH 58:6–8)

During the late 1990s, a major evangelical ministry was quite visible organizing national days of fasting and prayer. It even televised some of the events. (Ironically, Jesus counseled us on the Mount not to imitate "the hypocrites" but to pray in private and fast in a fashion so our neighbors will not know [Matthew 6:5–18]—and his original disciples did not bother to fast *at all* [Matthew 9:14].)

Admirable though the ministry's intent was, at the same time, evangelical author Philip Yancey was writing a book about why no one he could find ever associated the word *evangelical* with the word *graceful*. Others were writing about evangelicals' lack of social conscience, not only in government policy decisions but in their giving and investing patterns. And, sociologist George Barna observed that the "problem with Christianity in America is not the content of the faith," as delineated by Isaiah in the Scripture above, but the "failure of its adherents to integrate the faith into their lifestyles."

If we truly seek God's blessings on our nation, let us fast the way God wants us to.

———————————————— ❧ ————————————————

A terrible and shocking thing has happened in the land:
prophets speak nothing but lies; priests rule as the prophets
command, and my people offer no objections.
But what will they do when it all comes to an end?
(JEREMIAH 5:30–31)

Many American Christians seem to believe that prophets are sent to warn nonbelievers. The Bible describes a quite different and far more difficult reality about true prophets. They are typically sent to warn God's chosen, often about false prophets and priests acting like "entertainers" in the midst of the chosen. Consider the following texts, which echo the passage in Jeremiah 5:

Everyone, great and small, tries to make money dishonestly; even prophets and priests cheat the people. (Jeremiah 6:13)

The prophets are telling lies in my name; I did not send them, nor did I give them any orders or speak one word to them. The visions they talk about have not come from me; their predictions are worthless things that they have imagined. (Jeremiah 14:14)

So my people crowd in to hear what you have to say, but they don't do what you tell them to do. Loving words are on their lips but they continue their greedy ways. To them you are nothing more than an entertainer.... But when all your words come true—and they will come true—then they will know that a prophet has been among them. (Ezekiel 33:31)

And so, keeping quiet in such evil times is the smart thing to do! (Amos 5:13)

The true biblical ethic suggests that true prophecy has little to do with entertaining bestsellers and popular commentaries. It has little to do with predictions that prove incorrect year after year, decade after decade. It has little to do with accepting such entertainment and incorrect predictions as being from God rather than from men and women. And, it has little to do with knowing all this is wrong but keeping quiet because we don't want to offend a fellow Christian. As Martin Luther King Jr. liked to quote, all it takes for evil to triumph is for good people to do nothing.

The moral is that if you must have a modern prophet, seek one who is more focused on the evil among God's people than among nonbelievers— one who has been correct from time to time. One who sounds like an echo of the prophets of the Bible.

I, the LORD, search the minds and test the hearts of men. I treat each according to the way he lives, according to what he does.

(JEREMIAH 17:10)

St. Francis of Assisi once paraphrased this passage by saying: "It's no use walking anywhere to preach unless our walking is our preaching."

As a Protestant, I believe in the concept of salvation by the grace of God and not by the works of humankind. Yet, I cannot take that concept to the extremes that some of my friends do—that is, to conclude works are not important to God. That would be a rather unbiblical view.

Jeremiah, and particularly James in the Christian Scriptures, make it quite clear that God *is* interested in our works, at least as a sign that our hearts, minds, and souls have been truly touched by God's grace. Notice that even Jesus later comments on the Mount, "Not everyone who *calls* me 'Lord, Lord,' will enter the kingdom of heaven, but only those who *do* what my Father in heaven wants them to *do*" (Matthew 7:21, emphasis added).

My limited study of Luther, who first articulated the theology of salvation by grace and not works in its modern sense, even indicates that he believed our outer works to be a clear sign of our interior condition. He once said: "Good works do not make a man good; But a good man does good works."

That is, even an evil person who earns a fortune by evil means can make a small and public philanthropic donation and seem to be doing a good work. But that doesn't really make that person good. Yet someone whose heart, soul, and mind have truly been transformed by the graceful love of God simply *must* do good works as a regular part of the daily routine.

Unfortunately, Bill Bright, the founder of Campus Crusade, made this observation as the last millennium came to a close: "Even the Church, which has been the most trustworthy of institutions, has been greatly infiltrated by the ways of the world. Today, according to recent surveys, the Church is experiencing immorality, divorce and other tragic indications of disintegration just like the society in which it exists."

Sounding as blunt as Luther often seemed, Cal Thomas has added: "America's major social problems are a result of a rupture between faith and works. It isn't the fault of government. It isn't the fault of 'secular humanists.' Much of the fault can be put at the feet of the undisciplined, biblically ignorant, disobedient, uninformed, uncommitted, lethargic church."

They will throw their gold and silver away in the streets like garbage, because neither their silver nor gold can save them when the LORD *pours out his fury. They cannot use it to satisfy their desires or fill their stomachs. Gold and silver led them into sin.*

(EZEKIEL 7:19)

Here we see a representative passage indicating a further shift in the biblical perspective concerning wealth. We have moved from a seemingly direct connection between wealth and righteousness often found in the words of Moses to the nuanced view in Job and now to a view that gold and silver have actually led the people *astray,* into the fury of God.

This more prophetic view is somewhat closer to the view held by some ancient Greek philosophers. For example, in contrast to Jewish philosophers, Plato saw wealth and virtue as being on opposite ends of a balance scale. The more virtue, the less wealth. The less wealth, the more virtue.

Ezekiel's perspective begins to point toward the reality taught by Jesus. While it is not impossible for a virtuous person to obtain wealth, it is quite difficult, requiring considerable study and prayer to prevent that wealth from destroying virtue.

John Wesley may have summarized this paradoxical "protestant dilemma" with these words, as found in *Thoughts Upon Methodism*: "I fear, wherever riches have increased, (exceeding few are the exceptions,) the essence of religion, the mind that was in Christ, has decreased to the same proportion. Therefore do I not see how it is possible, in the nature of things, for any revival of true religion to continue for long. For religion must necessarily produce both industry and frugality; and these cannot but produce riches. But as riches increase, so will pride, anger, and love of the world in all its branches."

"As surely as I am the living God," the sovereign LORD *says, "your sister Sodom and her villages never did the evil that you and your villages have done. She and her daughters were proud because they had plenty to eat and lived in peace and quiet, but they did not take care of the poor and the underprivileged."*
(EZEKIEL 16:48)

This passage has always struck me as a most challenging one. For I expect if most people were asked what they want out of life, they might say "To have enough and to live in peace and quiet." Yet the prophet tells us that is exactly enough to get us destroyed. We are called to break out of our personal peace and quiet and take up the cause of the poor and underprivileged. Otherwise, we're actually worse in our sins of omission than those who live in more notable sins of commission.

Yet despite its challenging nature, this passage is reflective of the core teachings of Jesus, such as his Golden Rule. Many religions express a similar principle, but their versions are often simply opposed to doing harm to others. In contrast, the teaching of Jesus insists that we must not only avoid doing harm but actually do good, such as spending some of our time caring for those who are in need. Society may be enriched when we avoid doing harm, but we can find spiritual joy and meaning in life only when we engage in doing good.

--------------------------------- ✍ ---------------------------------

When they sow the wind, they will reap a storm!
(HOSEA 8:7)

Do we get what we deserve, or what our gracious God gives us despite what we deserve?

The answer to that question is yes! That is, we apparently get both on occasion. That complex reality was perhaps most famously captured in Reinhold Niebuhr's famous "Serenity Prayer," which says:

> God, grant me serenity to accept the things I cannot change,
> courage to change the things I can,
> and the wisdom to know the difference:
> Living one day at a time,
> accepting hardship as the pathway to peace,
> taking, as Jesus did,
> this sinful world as it is,
> not as I would have it;
> trusting that you will make all things right,
> if I surrender to your will,
> so that,
> I may be reasonably happy in this life and
> supremely happy with you forever in the next.

--------------------------------- ✍ ---------------------------------

"I knew that you are a loving and merciful God, always patient,
always kind, and always ready to change your mind and not punish.
Now then, LORD, let me die. I am better off dead than alive."
The LORD answered, "What right do you have to be angry?"
(JONAH 4:3–4)

In Jonah we glimpse Israel's changing perspective of God. Israel was maturing in the transitional era between the Jewish and Christian Scriptures. God was increasingly seen in a positive and loving sense rather than a negative and wrathful sense. God was even seen in a more humane sense, to the point of having a flexible divine mind that could be reasoned with by the prophets, rather than the distant mind who handed down absolutes from above.

This passage is also a caution to those of us who minister. Anyone who has been in ministry for a decade or more, particularly in a ministry of money, knows that ministry can be a most frustrating experience. As Upton Sinclair once remarked: "It's difficult to get a man to understand something when his salary depends on his not understanding it." In the mid-nineteenth century, the great British reformer Lord Shaftsbury tried to get Brits to understand that their cheap coal depended on thousands of children who were young enough and small enough to crawl around beneath the earth's surface. They often took their clothes off beneath ground due to the heat. Of course, there was an explosion of illegitimate children. But most Christians could not understand the root of the problem because no respectable Brit ever looked down the shafts of the mines. So Shaftsbury had to draw pictures for them. It's a bit like that today as those of us who might reform capitalism ask our clients to "look down the shafts" of their mutual funds to where their wealth is mined. It's not always a pretty picture to see that we own most of the industries our ministries resist. So most investors just don't look.

Like Jonah, we reformers can become so frustrated and even angry that we're tempted to ask God to rain a bit of fire on the church, just as many angry Christians attempted to create sparks on Capitol Hill during the 1990s. And, we may sulk as Jonah did when God uses those sparks to warm people's hearts rather than to burn their city. But, do we have any more right to question God's workings than Jonah did? Do we have the right to expect God to do our will rather than God's will and thereby turn our anger into joy? Probably not.

About the time America was being founded as a nation, Father Jean-Pierre de Caussade wrote a book that I've grown to treasure as I've continued my frustrating efforts. The translated title is *The Joy of Full Surrender*. It provides this gem for us willful ministers whose tendency is to seek God through the intellect and too often use that intellect to angrily argue with God:

> When God speaks it is a mystery, and therefore a death-blow to the senses and
> my reason, for it is the nature of mysteries to confound both. Mystery makes

the soul live by faith; everything else sees it as nothing but a contradiction. God's action by one and the same stroke kills and give life: the more one feels the death to the senses and reason, the more convinced should we become that it is bringing life to the soul. The darker the mystery the more light it contains. The life of faith is a continual struggle against the senses.

For the nonmystic, I will try to put that in the language of the great secular religion: golf. There is actually a fascinating book entitled *Golf in the Kingdom*. It is about a typical golfer who makes the pilgrimage to the mecca of golf. Transfixed by the wonders of his surroundings, he begins to play the round of a lifetime. After a few holes, he even begins to think he may even set the course record. But of course, he eventually makes a bad shot. And that brings his *emotions* into his game, particularly anger. Worse, he begins to *think* about his swing. And as all golfers know, the golf swing is so fast no one can think about it. The more you think, the worse it gets. Eventually, the golfer is ready to quit the game completely. To which his spiritually astute caddie replies: "Let the nothingness creep into your swing." And of course, now that the golfer is to the point of *surrender*, he finishes the round with some of his best golf ever. Having faith in our God, or our swing, is our only hope as the events of life move faster and faster.

Everyone will live in peace among his own vineyards and fig trees,
and no one will make him afraid.
(MICAH 4:4)

I believe that it is simply wrong to maintain that God and the Bible favor one modern form of economic organization, such as capitalism or socialism, over the other. The Bible clearly teaches concepts that should move the most conservative *and* most liberal readers far beyond their comfort zones and far above worldly approaches.

Yet in this passage, Micah seems to long for the day when each and every person has his or her own property and is free from both want and fear. This would imply that some economic structures might be more in tension with God's plan, or at least God's ideal for the future, than others. Let me use an agricultural metaphor to illustrate the plans the world has experimented with during the past century:

Feudalism: You have two cows. The lord of the castle takes some fresh milk and half the cheese.

Fascism: You have two cows. The government takes both, hires you to take care of them, and sells you the milk.

Communism: You have two cows. You must take care of them, but the government takes all the milk.

Casino Capitalism: You have two cows. You borrow 80 percent of the value of the two cows from your bank and buy other cows with 5 percent down. Then you sell the cows to a publicly listed company, which titles them with its tax-haven subsidiary in Bermuda. To buy the cows, it arranges a letter of credit that allows them to "put" the cows back to you if the price of milk falls by 20 percent. You enter retirement unsure of who really owns the cows and live in fear of falling milk prices.

Responsible Capitalism: You have two cows. You sell one and buy a bull. Your herd multiplies, and there's enough milk for you and your neighbors. You eventually sell the cows and retire during your old age, living in peace and security on the income of your past labors.

ↄ

What shall I bring to the LORD, the God of heaven, when I come
to worship him? Will the LORD be pleased if I bring him
thousands of sheep or endless streams of olive oil? No, the LORD has
told us what is good. What he requires of us is this: to do what is just,
to show constant love, and to live in humble fellowship with our
God. (MICAH 6:6–8)

A curse is on all of you because the whole nation is cheating me.
Bring the full amount of your tithes to the temple, so that there will
be plenty of food there. Put me to the test and you will see that
I will open the windows of heaven and pour out on you
in abundance all kinds of good things.

(MALACHI 3:9–10)

Attend most stewardship meetings of the church and odds are quite good that you will hear the second passage. Odds are equally good that you will not hear the first passage found on the previous page.

But, as we study the Scriptures, we see that Jesus, Moses, and the prophets were most probably far more interested in our doing what is just, showing constant love, and living in humble fellowship than in our bringing in the full amount of the tithe, terribly important though giving has been since the day God first created a world to give to us.

We should then notice that in the second, often-quoted but often-misunderstood passage from Malachi, God was not so much telling the people to fund the institutional needs of the temple but to make plenty of food available there for those in need. The temple did accept a small tax or donation for its needs, but this passage is about the temple also being a storehouse where all God's people could go in times of need.

During the twentieth century, the American church shifted more and more of that responsibility to government. There are now signs, such as the White House Office of Faith-based Initiatives, that government may shift some of the responsibility back toward the church, which is what Peter Drucker anticipated in *Post-Capitalist Society*. So, to move a little closer toward the biblical ideal of the storehouse in my own congregation, I recently asked my church council to establish a "revolving loan fund." It would be funded by donations in order to make small "soft" loans—which are repaid when possible but not pressed when repayment would burden the borrower—of a couple hundred dollars to members and nonmembers alike.

My church has an affluent but very social-minded congregation. Still, I was surprised by the high level of interest in the program. I was also surprised when some members of our church council said they knew of members who could use such a service. One even confessed she could have used it recently herself after losing her job. Frankly, I had had no idea someone I cared about had been in temporary need.

Such a fund, and similar ideas, might make our churches more relevant for the typical Christian. They might also be economic points of light for non-Christians who wonder what earthly good our churches are for.

Part III

The Spirit of the Christian Scriptures

"Tranquility is the soul of creativity."
Robert H. Schuller

CHAPTER SEVEN

THE FINANCIAL CHALLENGES
OF THE GOSPELS

"Orthodox Jews never have despised business; Christians have. . . . Getting rich has never been regarded as being in any way sinful, degrading or morally dubious within the Jewish religion, so long as such wealth is acquired legally and used responsibly. . . . It was generally assumed that the spirit of commerce is perfectly compatible with full religious faith and full religious practice. I think this is true in Islam as well, but it is not true in Christianity. . . . This difference gives Christianity certain immense advantages over both Judaism and Islam in terms of spiritual energy; but in its application to the practical world, it creates enormous problems."

Irving Kristol, *The Spiritual Roots of Capitalism and Socialism*

———————————————— ∽ ————————————————

"So if you are about to offer your gift to God at the altar and there
you remember that your brother has something against you, leave
your gift there in front of the altar, go at once and make peace with
your brother, and then come back to offer your gift to God."
(MATTHEW 5:23)

IN CHAPTER SIX we considered the last two prophetic passages of the Jewish Scriptures together because they foretold a key point Jesus would make on the Mount: From a higher perspective, giving is *never, ever* to clear our conscience by relieving us of our social responsibilities in the marketplace. Or, in the more modern vernacular: God doesn't want "conscience money," even if too many of our churches and ministries don't seem to mind it.

There was a time when churches were quite careful not to accept "tainted" money. But today, you're more likely to hear the rationalization of a more modern and well-known religious leader who said, "It's been the devil's money long enough; it's God's turn now" than to hear this particular teaching of Jesus. As such, it's simply another example of how the disciples of all the spiritual masters tend to distort the message of the master.

Later in his ministry, Jesus began Holy Week by using a whip to cleanse the temple of the moneychangers. Was that an indication of how, until a nation's church gets the seriousness of how the "root of all evil" can infiltrate even its sanctuaries, it will be difficult for that nation to get its priorities straight?

I think so. For Jesus could just as easily have said: "So, if you begin to fast, and you remember that your brother has something against you" or "So, if you begin to pray. . . ." Or, he could have begun Holy Week by using a whip to cleanse the palace, houses of prostitution, and other dens of iniquity. But he didn't. On the Mount, he connected a guilty conscience to the act of giving, because he knew that's how most of us would choose to assuage guilt. During Holy Week, he chastised those who took advantage of people's need to give.

As the prophets foretold, Jesus clearly preferred clean hearts, souls, and minds to tithes, especially tainted tithes.

For he makes his sun to shine on bad and good people alike, and
gives rain to those who do good and to those who do evil.
(MATTHEW 5:45)

Does God bless the righteous, as the books of Moses implied, or do evil people prosper, as Job and the prophets lamented? Yes.

The economic reality of the Jewish Scriptures, as summarized by Jesus in this passage, is that we serve a gracious God who gives to bad and good alike. It is what we do with those gifts, represented as money, that distinguishes mammon from the tithe.

But, no act of righteousness can earn the sun that warms us, the stars that light our nights, the oxygen that fills our lungs, or the water that sustains life itself. They are simply the beautiful gifts of a gracious God.

I hope that manifold grace toward my fellow sinners and those of other faiths has been the predominant theme of this book. For I believe it is the major characteristic of our loving God. Yes, I know that Christ himself said, "No one comes to the Father but by me." And I believe that. If someone seeks union with the perfect Father, he or she will simply have to live a life in imitation of Christ.

But, as a Lutheran, that may not be the central issue concerning salvation for me. I believe salvation is by the graceful coming of God to me, through Christ, not my going to the Father. And I don't want to limit God's grace in any way by implying that union with God is through our activities. As Jesus responded to the thief on the cross, our graceful God may surely save anyone God wants to save.

In short, it is not the intention of this book to give you an economic formula for getting into heaven. It is my intention to get heaven into you by having you accept the graceful love of God and by having that grace flow toward your neighbors.

I have faith that this will be quite adequate to assure the abundant life.

"Make certain that you do not perform your religious duties in public so that people will see what you do. If you do these things publicly, you will not have any reward from your Father in heaven. So when you give something to a needy person, do not make a big show of it, as the hypocrites do in the houses of worship."

(MATTHEW 6:1)

It is not at all unusual for churches to begin an annual stewardship campaign with "testimonies" about how much this person or that person has given. It is almost mandatory for the board members of Christian colleges to offer such testimony at the beginning of a capital campaign. It often seems that few are aware of the passage above. Or if they are aware, they basically ignore it in the pragmatism of the moment.

Of course, this passage does have to be balanced with the passage about not hiding one's good deeds beneath a basket so that no one can see them. Yet this should at least make us particularly humble when describing our giving, particularly to those in need.

It should also make us reflect always on these words from C. S. Lewis, as he shared them in *The Business of Heaven*:

> There have always been some who say, "The best good action is charity. The best kind of charity is giving money. The best thing is to give to is the Church. So hand us over ten thousand pounds and we will see you through." The answer to that nonsense, of course, would be that good actions done for that motive, done with the idea that Heaven can be bought, would not be good actions at all, but only commercial speculations.

While I certainly have nothing against a church or ministry being a good steward, C. S. Lewis knew that they should never, ever "operate more like a business" in that sense.

"So do not start worrying: 'Where will my food come from?
or my drink? or my clothes?' These are the things the pagans are
always concerned about. Your Father in heaven knows that you need
all these things. Instead, be concerned above everything else with
the Kingdom of God and with what he requires of you,
and he will provide you with all these other things. So do not worry
about tomorrow: it will have enough worries of its own.
There is no need to add to the troubles each day brings."
(MATTHEW 6:31–34)

If I had to cite one concept that summarizes the economic approach of the Bible, it would be the paradoxical statement to: "Seek first the kingdom and all this shall be added unto you." Such paradox is difficult for all of us. But it is even more difficult for some Christians. In the April 22, 2002 edition of *Christianity Today*, Professor John Stackhouse confessed: "Evangelicalism generally eschews paradox. We prefer the clarity of binary opposition, and there are many such pairs in the Bible; light versus darkness, good versus evil, the kingdom of God versus the kingdom of Satan, the church versus the world, the flesh versus the Spirit. Yet we are Bible people, and we must listen also to Scriptures that speak of the kingdom itself as a 'mixed field' (Mt. 13:24–30), full of wheat and tares, and of the Christian life as being in the world but not of it . . . We might recognize that God has called us to lives of difficult paradox, of painful negotiation between conflicting and competitive values, of seeking to cooperate with God wherever he is at work. Such a position, full of ambiguity and irony, is also full of faith and hope." The passage from the Sermon on the Mount is essentially an elaboration on such a paradox. It contains several economic and spiritual realities:

1. There is no need to worry about the economic future. If there is something you can do to change it, you will, and so there is no need to worry in the first place. If there is nothing you can do to change it, worrying won't help!

2. If there is indeed something in the economic future worth worrying about, you can be assured there will be enough "pagans" around to worry about it, particularly in our culture, which seems to value material riches more than spiritual riches. Some of us tried to point this out during the federal debt and Y2K "crises." When the debt looked like it might become a problem, even secular politicians and voters turned their attention to it. That attention and the end of the Cold War kept the debt from becoming even a problem, much less the crisis that many imagined it might be. The same was true with Y2K. A significant percentage of the computer programmers in the world were busy working on the problem. There was no need for some followers of Jesus to appear more worried about the problem than most anyone around.

3. God knows our every need, probably better than we do, since we often confuse needs with wants and desires.

4. Our concern should be about what God requires of *us*, not of politicians and computer programmers. As this passage indicates, God particularly requires us to focus on the present spiritual kingdom, not on projections of future material shortages. This makes

particular sense, as those most worried about future shortages tend to hoard their seed today. They thereby avoid planting for the future, in turn making their worst fears about shortages a reality.

5. Be assured that every tomorrow will have something to worry about. While Christians are to live in the spiritual kingdom, we know we will never live in an earthly Utopia, as promised by Karl Marx on the left and Ayn Rand on the right.

All God requires of us is to grow spiritually until we can handle today's problems as mature believers should.

"Do not think that I have come to bring peace to the world.
No, I did not come to bring peace, but a sword."
(MATTHEW 10:34)

If I had to name the greatest threats to your future abundant life, a global war would rank very near the top. And if I had to name one concern that might prompt a global war after the fall of the Berlin Wall, it would be the tensions between the West and Islam.

As history has proven time and again, religion brings out not only the best in people but the worst in people. And since religion, whether theistic or nontheistic, is always about ultimate values, it is the one area that people should always be ready to die for. That is why it is imperative that we get religion right.

This verse in Matthew 10 is one example of why we should be most careful and most gracious when we casually read the scriptures of the other great faiths, many of which were also written in ancient times and in far different cultures. For, contrary to what many Americans might say today, this text was spoken by Jesus and not Muhammad.

Yet as this manuscript went off to the editors, the newspapers were reporting that a group of conservative, politically-inclined religious leaders were pressuring President Bush, having concluded that the Qur'an proves Islam is a "violent" religion. One prominent Christian radio commentator has even extracted the "violent" passages for his listeners and readers. I do not argue whether the *selected* passages indicate that Islam has a too-often violent history. But, if we are to take the log out of Christianity's eye, we must admit that isolated passages from the Bible, and particularly from the older Jewish Scriptures, might easily prove to the other world faiths that our faith is also a violent religion.

God knows that the disciples of Jesus, starting with Peter at the arrest of Jesus, have relied far too heavily upon the sword. And the world surely knows that "Christian" America spends as much on swords than other nations combined. But God also knows that when Christianity is read in context, the earliest Jewish texts reflect a primitive understanding of God and the teachings of Christ concerning the sword are a metaphor for how the spirit of God would cleanly sever forever those who hate from those who love.

Yes, it is the greatest act of love for us to share our faith with those of other faiths. But let us be as gracious toward their faith and their sacred texts as we would like for them to be toward ours. And let us remember that Jews, Muslims, and Christians share the Pentateuch, which is a common economic language for living together on this earth.

"The seeds that fell on rocky ground stand for those who receive the message gladly as soon as they hear it. But it does not sink deep into them, and they don't last long. So when trouble or persecution comes because of the message, they give up at once."

(MATTHEW 13:20–21)

Throughout this book—indeed, throughout the last decade—I have tried to help investors understand that the surest way to make money is to act in a counterintuitive way when "trouble or persecution" comes along. Generally, this means to go the opposite direction of where all one's neighbors seem to be going with their investments.

After witnessing examples such as the federal debt and Y2K, most people mentally assent that the approach works. But it doesn't sink very deeply into the hearts and minds of the vast majority. For when trouble or persecution arises again—and we've been assured on the Mount that such trials will come—we tend to follow our intuitions and join the crowd.

I often teach young people my "10–20–40–500" rule. It says that if you can earn 10 percent on your money (which is less than the stock market has averaged during the modern era), saving $20 per week for the 40 years that most people work during their careers, then you will retire with $500,000.

Many young people enthusiastically begin such a program after my seminars. But then a little "trouble or persecution" hits their portfolios or an advertiser suggests a more "enriching" approach to life, and they discontinue the program. They never get to discover that the laws of compounding insist that a large percentage of the rewards are delivered during the last ten years of the program. (To demonstrate this law to your children, ask if they'd like a million dollars or a penny to be doubled each day for a month. Do the exercise with them and have them notice that for twenty days, they appear to have made a mistake if they took the penny. It is only during the last ten days that the wonders of compounding become evident. It works much the same way with the years of a life as with the days of a month.)

In much the same way, during my seminars mature investors often respond enthusiastically to ethical, socially responsible, values-based, or spiritual investing. But they typically return to their own financial advisor, who is rarely knowledgeable in the area, and he or she explains all the "troubles" with actually implementing the approach. My message about the merits of spirituality and ethics doesn't sink in.

"The Kingdom of heaven is like this. A man happens to find
a treasure hidden in a field. . . . A man is looking for fine pearls. . . .
Some fishermen throw their net out in the lake and catch all kinds
of fish. . . . 'Do you understand these things?'
Jesus asked them. 'Yes,' they answered."
(MATTHEW 13:44–51)

Jesus was not talking simply about treasure, pearls, and fish. He was at least marginally, and probably largely, using the material wealth that people val-

ued to communicate spiritual principles they might not otherwise understand. And although his disciples failed to understand most of the things
Jesus spoke about most of the time, they clearly understood what he was
saying this time!

Now imagine America's ministers, both ordained and lay, explaining the
kingdom of God to our money culture this way: "The kingdom of heaven is
like a patient and socially responsible mutual fund that lovingly seeks to prudently enrich our neighbors as ourselves.... It's like a community development bank that pays us a reasonable rate of return as it lovingly develops
housing and jobs for the less fortunate in our inner cities.... It is like a
microlending ministry that helps wealthy North Americans lovingly create
tiny jobs for the least of these around the world...." The growing money
cultures of the world just might understand.

In one of my favorite modern passages, Professor Jon P. Gunnemann has
written in *Religion and Values in Public Life*:

> Jesus surely drew on so many economic examples because they were imme-
> diately intelligible to his hearers. It is not much different today. The eyes of
> your listeners are less likely to glaze over if you talk about capital, dividends,
> and interest than if you talk about the incarnation, the trinity and the two
> natures of Christ. It "pays" to use economic language in order to communi-
> cate clearly, and the reason is that economics is not just one dimension of
> existence; it refers to the entire household of the world—what the poet Wen-
> dell Berry called "The Great Economy."

That is why I find it particularly tragic that Christian ministers who do the
most talking about economics through our media often talk the most economic nonsense.

---

*Jesus said to him, "If you want to be perfect, go and sell all you have
and give the money to the poor, and you will have riches in heaven;
then come and follow me." When the young man heard this,
he went away sad, because he was very rich.*

(MATTHEW 19:21)

This text is commonly known as the story of the rich young ruler. It precedes Jesus' famous teaching that it is easier for a camel to pass through the eye of the needle than for a rich man to enter the kingdom of God.

When isolated from the other teachings of Jesus, this text often leaves the impression that Jesus was starting a new religion, one that rejected the early Jewish thought that material riches are a blessing of God. But as we shall see later in our study, there were wealthy disciples of Jesus described in what we now call the Christian Scriptures. Not many perhaps, but some. And so, the teaching about the eye of the needle was followed by Jesus' explanation that "what is impossible for man is possible with God," indicating that if a rich person has been blessed with the grace of God, even he or she might make it into the kingdom. It may even be easier in our modern economy.

Yet, we should also be clear that there are other passages of the Christian Scriptures which seem nearly as ascetic (i.e., embracing of absolute poverty) as this one. For example, we are told that when Mary was still pregnant with Jesus, she sang, "He has filled the hungry with good things and sent the rich away with empty hands." Luke 12:32–33 says that Jesus later taught: "Do not be afraid, little flock, for your Father is pleased to give you the Kingdom. Sell all your belongings and give the money to the poor."

In short, Jesus acknowledged both the difficulties and nuances of wealth. During more than two decades of studying books and human nature, I've observed how much stress and anxiety most people can experience when accumulating and managing wealth. But I've also met a few people who, like Sir John Templeton, seem to handle the heavy responsibilities of wealth management with the lightness of angels. And I've met a few people, for example the "little flock" of Mother Teresa's and other saints, who were blessed to take these passages most literally.

As for me, I readily confess that I will never "be perfect" as the rich young man aspired to be. Not being a saint, this disciple has chosen a path of moderation, pursing a materially and spiritually balanced life. In recent years, I have worked hard at attaining wealth that is moderate—by Wall Street's standard if not by the standards of the Bible and the world—while doing my best not to lose my soul. Was it the wisest of choices? In hindsight, possibly not. As the saying goes, few people lie on their deathbeds wishing they had spent more time in the office. And I continue to notice that I'm rarely as happy when I'm working and making very good money than I am when I have lost myself in my writing and teaching.

Like most people I know, I now feel I have spent too many of my previous days foolishly pursuing matters that now seem mostly unimportant in the scheme of things. But as the adage observes, youth is often wasted on the young. Fortunately, life is often equally cherished by the old.

——————————————— ✍ ———————————————

Jesus said to them, "I tell you the publicans and harlots are going into the kingdom of heaven before you."
(MATTHEW 21:31)

When I began writing this book a couple years ago, I had decided to be as honest as possible about how the economic nonsense spewing from the Christian media was hindering some of our efforts at developing the kingdom of God on earth. Many times since, I have wondered if I have grown overly skeptical, even cynical. But as I edit this manuscript for the final time, a friend has just e-mailed me the results of a survey conducted by Barna Research, perhaps the most authoritative observer of the evangelical subculture. It began:

> One reason why evangelical churches across the nation are not growing is due to the image that non-Christian adults have of evangelical individuals. In a nationwide survey among a representative sample of people who do not consider themselves to be Christian, the image of "evangelicals" rated tenth out of eleven groups evaluated, beating out only prostitutes. The non-Christian population was not as dismissive of all Christians or religious people, however, as ministers and "born-again Christians" were among the three highest-rated segments evaluated.

By the grace of God, financial advisors weren't included. But the groups and the percentage of non-Christians viewing them favorably were:

Military officer	56%
Ministers	44%

Born-again Christians	32%
Democrats	32%
Real estate agents	30%
Movie & TV performers	25%
Lawyers	24%
Republicans	23%
Lesbians	23%
Evangelicals	22%
Prostitutes	5%

Another example of media perceptions creating a false reality?

———————————————— ↄ ————————————————

"How terrible for you, teachers of the Law and Pharisees! You hypocrites! You give to God one tenth even of the seasoning herbs, such as mint, dill and cumin, but you neglect to obey the really important teachings of the Law, such as justice and mercy and honesty. These you should practice, without neglecting the others. Blind guides! You strain a fly out of your drink, but swallow a camel!"

(MATTHEW 23:23–24)

As the last millennium came to a close, *The Economist* magazine published a full page "Obituary for Jesus." It remarked that the church may now insist that Christians must believe in only one thing—that Jesus rose from the dead. But it was only partially correct: Most churches still ask Christians to believe in giving to the church.

While there's nothing wrong with teaching that we should give to the church—Jesus seemed to strongly endorse it when he admired the woman and her two mites—the very strong language in Matthew 23 should give every church leader pause. The reality is that God never made it part of the Law of Moses that believers would be executed for failing to tithe. But, God did make it part of the law that those who did not manage their livestock investments in ways that did no harm to their neighbors would be executed (Exodus 21:28).

Clearly, the Law of Moses affirmed that the responsible management of wealth was at least equally as important as tithing. The law acknowledged that we would never discover the abundant life if we made money by hurting others and then gave to heal them. Yet today, we almost never hear of the first principle, although we often hear of the second.

Could we also be "blind guides?" Of course we are. Fortunately, the grace of God assures that we are beloved blind guides. That grace of God should open our eyes as will our wallets.

"I was afraid, so I went off and hid your money in the ground. Look! Here is what belongs to you." "You bad and lazy servant!" his master said. "You knew, did you, that I reap harvests where I did not plant, and gather crops where I did not scatter seed? Well, then, you should have deposited my money in the bank, and I would have received it all back with interest when I returned. Now, take the money away from him and give it to the one who has ten thousand coins. For to every person who has something, even more will be given, and he will have more than enough; but the person who has nothing, even the little that he has will be taken away from him. As for this useless servant—throw him outside in the darkness; there he will cry and gnash his teeth."

(MATTHEW 25:25–30)

Commonly called the parable of the talents, this passage in Matthew 25 could just as easily be called the great parable of capitalism. It describes two difficult realities often associated with a market economy. First, life may be good but it isn't fair. We are not all given the same time, talents, treasure, and opportunities in life. Second, which is a result of the first, what counts is what we do with what we have been given. While we may not be rewarded equally in *material* ways, we are apparently rewarded in equal ways *spiritually* when we faithfully use the little or much we have been given.

We are told that the owner of property goes on a long trip and leaves his property in the care of three stewards. We are also told that the owner does not entrust an equal share to each of the three stewards but an unequal amount "according to his ability." The two most able stewards, those with the greatest resources, multiplied what they had been given. We are told that when they render an accounting to the master upon his return, the master invites them to join in his happiness—the spiritual reward.

But the third was "afraid," and thus he buried, or hoarded, the little that he had been given, all the while rationalizing that he was surely doing what the master would have him to do. Ironically, that's almost exactly what tens of thousands of Christians believed when filling church basements full of food and fuel for Y2K . . . while also expecting the imminent return of the master.

Yet, the master surprises the fearful steward, telling him that he could have at least put the money with bankers and earned a little interest. That wasn't considered a particularly creative or righteous form of stewardship in the community. But Jesus seemed to prefer it to fearfully hoarding God's resources. The truly tragic part of the parable, however, is not the losing of a bit of interest. It is the losing of a soul, for Jesus himself says the fearful steward will be cast "outside in the darkness; there he will cry and gnash his teeth."

We might also notice that Jesus immediately goes on to describe what we call the final judgment. As I have described before, that text says we will be judged not according to what we believe. Even Satan believes in God and that Jesus was God's Son. We will be judged according to whether our beliefs were strong enough that we put them into action by using God's resources to feed the hungry, give drink to the thirsty, and cloth the naked.

When it was evening, a rich man from Arimathea arrived: his name was Joseph, and he also was a disciple of Jesus.
(MATTHEW 27:57)

Jesus clearly taught that it is most difficult for rich people to enter the kingdom of heaven. Yet the Bible also clearly assures us that entry for the rich isn't impossible. In fact, this passage in Matthew 27 indicates that Jesus was buried in the tomb of a wealthy disciple.

Some theologians have read special meaning in the irony of contrasting Jesus' assertion that the love of money is the root of all evil with the historical reality that a rich man played a major role in the scene of the last and greatest triumph of the Christian faith. For example, Jacques Ellul wrote this passage in his wonderful book entitled *Money and Power*:

> The total consecration of money to God is a prophetic act because it announces the last days. It is an element of the kingdom of heaven in the midst of us, announcing the greater and final reality of God's kingdom. It is an element of the kingdom of heaven because it means that God's grace is worth giving up everything for. But this renunciation does not mean leaving things to go their own way; it does not in any sense mean that money is given back to mammon. It is rather a surrender into God's hands, and thus it is a reintegration. For ultimately reintegration is what lies ahead for money, when the power of money admits its submission to Christ. This is one of the last-day promises in both Old and New Testaments.

As we have seen, the story of the rich young ruler suggests the last area of our lives that we will submit to Christ is our money—not our tithes, which even the rich young ruler had surrendered, but what we call "our money."

If we have "reintegrated" that most difficult of areas, the odds are quite good that the other areas of our lives are under Christ's lordship as well.

The obvious question, which should bedevil end-times theologians for some time to come, is: If the world were to get around to reintegrating its money with its faith, would the kingdom of God be realized? Perhaps even more importantly, for all of us, can it be realized until the world does?

———————————— ⁐ ————————————

Jesus returned from the Jordan full of the Holy Spirit and was led
by the Spirit into the desert, where he was tempted by the devil
for forty days. In all that time he ate nothing, so that he was hungry
when it was over. The Devil said to him, "If you are God's Son,
order this stone to turn into bread." But Jesus answered,
"The scripture says, 'Man cannot live on bread alone.'"

(LUKE 4:1–3)

It may be the first temptation of every Christian minister, and of every Christian financial minister in particular, to turn stones into bread for their followers. It is definitely the first temptation of Christian politicians and economists who are concerned with enriching the more material dimensions of life. As Malcolm Muggeridge once wrote:

> The Roman authorities distributed free bread to promote Caesar's kingdom, and Jesus could do the same to promote his. . . . Jesus had but to give a nod of agreement and he could have constructed Christendom, not on four shaky Gospels and a defeated man on a Cross, but on a basis of sound socioeconomic planning and principles. . . . Every utopia could have been brought to pass, every hope have been realized and every dream been made to come true. Acclaimed, equally, in the London School of Economics and the Harvard Business School: a statue in Parliament Square, and an even bigger one on Capitol Hill and in the Red Square. . . . Instead, he turned the offer down on the ground that only God should be worshipped.

"And if you lend only to those from whom you hope to get it back,
why should you receive a blessing? Even sinners lend to sinners,
to get back the same amount! No! Love your enemies and do good
to them; lend and expect nothing back. You will then have a great
reward, and you will be sons of the Most High God.
For he is good to the ungrateful and the wicked.
Be merciful just as your Father is merciful."
(LUKE 6:34–36)

Have you ever experienced the spiritual blessing of making a loan that others would think you foolish to make? No AAA credit rating. No government guarantees that you will get your principal back. No charity. Just helping someone in need both financially and spiritually by demonstrating that you love him or her enough and trust enough to extend credit. In a very real sense, that belief signals more confidence in the recipient than it would if the lender made a charitable donation for the person's need, because you have confidence in that person's ability to repay.

Maybe it's a desperately poor person in the Third World who needs to borrow $200 for a used sewing machine, and you lend that amount through a microenterprise ministry. Maybe it's someone in your church who just needs a helping hand to get over a short-term cash squeeze, and you make that loan personally or through your church's revolving loan fund. Maybe it's even a defeated and chaotic once-"evil" nation that many of your friends still deem to be the enemy, and you make a loan through a developing markets bond fund.

Be assured that people, particularly those of us who have been trained in credit analysis, will think you foolish. But, be equally assured that God will not. As Rabbi Professor Jonathan Sacks recently explained in *Religion and Liberty*:

> Judaism's strong provisions for *tzedakah* (a word meaning both charity and righteousness) are designed not only to alleviate poverty but also, and primarily, to restore independence. Hence, in Jewish law, the highest form of charity is to find someone a job so that he or she no longer needs to depend on charity.

In essence, the ancient concept of *tzedakah* asked God's people to make it a priority to create jobs for those who needed them, because that way of assisting the needy granted them the most dignity. *Tzedakah* then says to make loans to those who need them, because that demonstrates our confidence that they might eventually repay. Only then are we to give charity, and when possible, that is to be done so the poor do not even know from whom the charity is received. The next lowest level of *tzedakah* is to give when the needy know who we are.

In short, we who are wealthy are typically trained by our culture—and many church leaders—to look at helping those who need to borrow our excess wealth from *our perspectives as fortunate lenders*. We are told that we need to *give* for the good of our souls and we are often *recognized* for doing so publicly through our institutions.

But the biblical ethic reverses all that by teaching us to look at such matters *from the perspective of God's beloved needy*. They don't necessarily want the world knowing that we have helped them. And they don't necessarily feel love when it is channeled through institutions rather than given at the same time that our personal care is. When we give both care and money, the spiritual rewards flow to both donor and recipient. Any earthly rewards to the donor, and they are occasionally most substantial, are still purely a byproduct and received without expectation.

John spoke up, "Master we saw a man driving out demons in your name, and we told him to stop, because he doesn't belong to our group." "Do not try to stop him," Jesus said to him and to the other disciples, "because whoever is not against you is for you."

(LUKE 9:49–50)

The November 18, 2002 issue of *Christianity Today* contained an interview with Franklin Graham, whom I respect, who said: "After 9/11, there were groups that said we all worship the same God. It's not the same God. The God of Islam is not a father. The God of the Christian faith is a father. He has a son; his name is Jesus." The next issue of *CT* interviewed my friend Tony Campolo, who quoted the Scripture above as an indicator that Christians might work with those of other faiths. Lots of Christians were surely confused about how they should interact with Islam.

It probably won't surprise you that I see truth in both views. On a purely theological level, I believe much of what Graham said—although I'm now more reluctant to claim that God must be masculine. And I think God has lots of children, of both genders, who go by many names, names that I hope include Gary and perhaps Muhammad.

I also greatly admire Tony's perspective. So I'm now going to make the most politically incorrect confession of this book: When it comes to purely secular affairs, those of us who worship our Creator by integrating our faith and wealth management most probably think more like most moderate Muslims seeking the kingdom of God than we do those extreme, compartmentalized Western Christians seeking the American Dream. Many might also consider it most incorrect to wonder if Christians should align themselves solidly in the same political party with noted atheists who detest our

God at the same time we indiscriminately declare our cousins of The Book to be the enemy. But I don't think Jesus would.

The point of this text in Luke 9 is that while Jesus wants his followers to remain faithful, he doesn't want us to stop others who are doing similar work in the world, such as integrating ethics and corporate behavior. To be pointed, remember how you felt on 9/11 when 3000 Americans were killed? Now imagine how foreign leaders feel when the cigarette industry I grew up in kills 400,000 people each and every year. Foreign governments are going to great lengths to keep that industry at bay. Yet the worst impulses of capitalism tempt the youth of those nations.

Careless, biblically uninformed words can not only discourage such work of God's people around the world, they can create the worst kind of conflict.

The teacher of the law wanted to justify himself,
so he asked Jesus, "Who is my neighbor?"
(LUKE 10:29)

It's not all that difficult to "love thy neighbor" as most of the world defines *neighbor*. After all, people who live next door probably *are* quite similar to one another.

And as an investment advisor, I have found that it's rarely all that difficult to love my clients, because their business helps me to care for the people, myself included, and organizations that I love. Yet, when I was suffering from burnout at the height of the junk bond fiasco of the late 1980s, I realized I wasn't all that different from prominent figures such as junk bond king Michael Milken. I too was taking care of my clients who came to me for advice on making more money. And I too was not conscious of those out-of-sight and out-of-mind people who were hurt by my activities. I discovered the real key to ethics lay in whom one identified as one's "neighbor."

During the years since, I've discovered that how we define *neighbor* is critically important regardless of the investments we make. *Every single investment we make affects our neighbors, properly defined, one way or another.*

Jesus made the concept of neighbor a universal one when he gave his life for the entire world, even those he had never met and thus would never benefit from. It was that kind of love that motivated New York police officers and firefighters to climb the smoking World Trade Center towers. It has been that ethic that has prompted many heroic soldiers to give their lives for their neighbors in battle.

Yet, more worldly philosophers often disagree. For example, in her book *The Virtue of Selfishness,* Ayn Rand wrote these words:

> It is only in emergency situations that one should volunteer to help strangers, if it's in one's power. For instance, a man who values human life and is caught in a shipwreck, should help to save his fellow passengers—though not at the expense of his own life. But this does not mean that after they all reach shore, he should devote his efforts to saving his fellow passengers from poverty, ignorance, neurosis, or whatever troubles they might have.

I believe the New York police and firefighters essentially taught us that America will feel better about itself when the chips are down and be much happier when the chips are up if we define *neighbor* with the more selfless ethic of Jesus rather than the more selfish ethic of Rand.

"The next day, he took out two silver coins and gave them to the innkeeper. 'Take care of him,' he told the innkeeper, 'and when I come back this way, I will pay you whatever else you spend on him.'"
(LUKE 10:35)

I occasionally hear a development officer suggest that it is unbiblical to establish trusts and other planned gifts and that we should simply give our money now so we might meet all the current needs of our world. I assume they are well intentioned despite the obvious financial self-interest. (While church leaders are rarely financially astute, they do understand that a dollar today is more valuable than a dollar tomorrow!) But, I also wonder if they have ever thought about this in relation to the story of the Good Samaritan.

For, while the Good Samaritan did indeed care for the hurting man's current needs, the Samaritan also wisely provided for the needs the hurting man would have after the Samaritan had to move on. By leaving funds in the care of the innkeeper, the Samaritan essentially accomplished what many charitable trusts and foundations do today. By looking after the hurting man, the innkeeper essentially accomplished what many trustees do today. Some might counter that the Bible says we shouldn't put off until tomorrow what we should do today. I agree. But establishing a charitable trust today for tomorrow's needs *is* acting today.

The belief that we should do one or the other, but not both, probably indicates that we operate from a scarcity rather than abundance mentality. It may also indicate a lack of faith to say that we can set aside something for those in need tomorrow and still have enough for ourselves and others today.

Such will always be the beliefs of humanity, including religious humanity. Fortunately, the Bible encourages more godly, faith-filled beliefs.

Jesus came to a village where a woman named Martha welcomed him in her home. She had a sister named Mary, who sat down at the feet of the Lord *and listened to his teaching. Martha was upset over all the work she had to do, so she came and said, 'Lord, don't you care that my sister has left me to do all the work by myself? Tell her to come and help me!' The* Lord *answered her, 'Martha, Martha! You are worried and troubled over so many things, but just one is needed. Mary has chosen the right thing, and it will not be taken away from her.'*

(LUKE 10:38–42)

Human beings do not live by bread alone, even when that bread is made by the most devout, hard-working, and loving disciples.

Many theologians will tell you that too many American Christians have forgotten this very basic teaching far too often, usually with dire consequences. For example, many conservative theologians believe it was a crucial mistake for our mainline Christian denominations to focus on the so-called "social gospel" during the early twentieth century because they busied themselves building hospitals and soup kitchens, rather than evangelizing the world with the good news of Christ. Some liberal theologians believe it was an equal mistake later in the century for evangelicals to busy themselves broadcasting their perceptions of the federal debt and Y2K rather than discipling Christian business leaders in the financial ethics of Christ. In both cases, they agree the church erred in placing too much emphasis on material affairs rather than far more important spiritual and ethical matters.

That "material emphasis" was often the result of the church buying into secular philosophies. As the century came to a close, influential philosopher Ayn Rand taught that the moral purpose of our lives was "productive achievement." Many of us, including many believers, busied ourselves with making money, politics, filling churches with food and fuel for Y2K, and other questionable activities. Many leaders were running around prompting their followers to get so busy that they no longer seemed to have time to sit still for a while with Jesus. Ironically, the Bible reminds us that the "only" thing that was really needed was to do just that—sit for a while with the Christ Spirit.

As a physician, Luke was inclined to provide spiritual medicine to those in need. And many of his writings address the topic of money or the earning of money through "productive achievement." Those writings are a wonderful spiritual tonic for the money culture of the West.

A man in the crowd said to Jesus, "Teacher, tell my brother to divide with me the property our father left us." Jesus answered him, "Man, who gave me the right to judge or to divide the property between you two?" And he went on to say to them all, "Watch out and guard yourselves from every kind of greed."
(LUKE 12:13)

A request for seemingly simple economic justice. But it was understood by Jesus as simply another act of greed.

We don't know whether Jesus had special insight into the particular situation, insight that allowed him to make this judgment, or whether he was simply stating a general principle. But every reader of religious financial books who might become too focused on the economic justice advocated by the Jewish Scriptures should clearly understand that the way wealth is divided in this world was not a major concern of Jesus. This is particularly true of those individuals who are politically active in the private, public, and independent sectors who seem to believe their sector should always have a more "just" or larger share of the economic pie.

Jesus did not even use the opportunity for fundraising by suggesting the two brothers should just give the disputed property to the temple or the poor! That may be why Leonard Bacon wrote these words in *The Christian Doctrine of Stewardship* in 1832:

> The church was not formed to manage the property of its members, or to command their charitable efforts; nor can it show any commission to that effect. You are a steward not for the church but for God. The property which you have, or may have in possession, belongs to you; as an individual, and not as a member of the church; and you as an individual, must account for it to the supreme proprietor.

Yes, you probably purchased this book thinking that it would tell you how to manage wealth. By now, I hope you realize that it's actually about how to love God and neighbor as self. The paradox is that this is the best wealth management strategy I've learned in twenty-five years on the Street. Sir John Templeton believes it is the best strategy he has learned in seven decades of wealth management.

---

*Then Jesus told them this parable: "There was once a rich man who had land which bore good crops. . . . 'This is what I will do,' he told himself; 'I will tear down my barns and build bigger ones. . . .
Then I will say to myself, Lucky man! You have all the good things you need for many years. Take life easy, eat, drink, and enjoy yourself!' But God said to him, 'You fool! This very night you will have to give up your life; then who will get all these things you have kept for yourself?'" And Jesus concluded, "This is how it is with those who pile up riches for themselves but are not rich in God's sight."*

(LUKE 12:16–20)

We often hear that this passage is about building bigger barns. But count the times the words "barn" and "self" appear in the passage. It is actually far more about selfishness than bigger barns. The rich man was not concerned about using his wealth for the glory of God or for the benefit of his neighbors. He was concerned only for his own comfort. And it was that limited perspective, not the building of bigger barns, that was the death of his soul.

It's also important to note that the bigger barns were not simply temporary storage facilities to be used until the crops got to market, as we know them today. They were long-term storage facilities for one's own well-being. Bigger barns that facilitate the feeding of more neighbors are not forbidden in the Bible, even if the Christian Scriptures instruct us to not worry so much about them.

This passage is also *not* about sowing larger fields that might benefit humanity. In other words, Jesus was *not* sowing seeds of guilt and discouraging us from being productive members of society. He was simply condemning hoarding, discouraging us from trusting in our wealth, resting on our laurels, and thereby no longer being fruitful members of society.

As Henri Nouwen reminded us, since the days of The Garden, God has always taught that being "fruitful" and multiplying in material and spiritual ways is one of the very few true needs of humanity. We just have to keep those activities balanced and properly prioritized.

— ℘ —

"Do not be afraid, little flock, for your Father is pleased to give you the Kingdom. Sell all your belongings and give the money to the poor. Provide for yourselves purses that don't wear out, and save your riches in heaven, where they will never decrease, because no thief can get to them, and no moth can destroy them. For your heart will always be where your riches are."
(LUKE 12:32–34)

"Do not be afraid." Jesus knew that fear probably played a greater role in acquisitiveness and hoarding among the "little flock" he was addressing than greed does on the Wall Street we know today. But, he assured them—and us—God is most happy to provide what we really need, at least if the faith community is not caught up in hoarding.

When Jesus used the words "never decrease," he also taught that spiritual investing is the greatest risk/reward relationship of all time. It is an absolute win-win, can't-lose situation when you understand your gains can be more than financial.

And, notice that Jesus said our hearts will "always" follow our riches, not vice versa. Invest in a stock and see if you don't become more conscious of that company's activities, with your emotions rising and falling as its fortunes do. It works the same way when we "invest" in noncommercial endeavors.

During my career, I have seen less than perfect investors establish a charitable trust for the future benefit of a church, college, or ministry, often for the investor's tax or income needs—but then they grow appreciative of giving itself and of that institution. Their hearts often soften and their souls quicken, providing riches of far greater value than the tax savings they had originally sought.

"If then you have not been faithful in handling worldly wealth,
how can you be trusted with true wealth? No servant can be the slave
of two masters; he will hate one and love the other; he will be loyal
to one and despise the other. You cannot serve both God and money."
When the Pharisees heard all this, they made fun of Jesus
because they loved money.
(LUKE 16:11–14)

If we cannot understand the finances of our government, the internal workings of a computer, or the ethics of investing, can we be trusted with the meaning and purpose of life itself?

If we cannot speak intelligently about economic matters, can we evangelize our money culture with the following hard questions?

For whom do we work: God or money?

For whom do we invest: God or money?

Of whom do we think most of the time: God or money?

Whom do we worship: God or mammon, defined as money that is not infused with the spirit of love?

And, finally, when the world looks at us, whom does it see: The Son of God or the Pharisees who loved money? Both were religious. Both went to the temple on a regular basis. Both fasted. Both appreciated tithing. Both knew the difference between right and wrong.

But only one loved unconditionally in the difficult truth-filled way.

"The poor man died and was carried by the angels to sit beside Abraham at the feast in heaven. The rich man died and was buried, and in Hades, where he was in great pain, he looked up and saw Abraham, far away, with Lazarus at his side."

(LUKE 16:22–23)

St. Augustine once commented on this very difficult and often misunderstood story this way:

> Although the haughty and rich man who was clothed in purple and fine linen and feasted sumptuously every day died and was tormented in Hell, nevertheless, if he had shown mercy to the poor man covered with sores who lay at his door and was treated with scorn, he himself would have deserved mercy. And if the poor man's merit had been his poverty, not his goodness, he surely would not have been carried by angels into the bosom of Abraham. On the one hand, it was not poverty in itself that was divinely honored, nor, on the other, riches that were condemned, but that the godliness of the one and the ungodliness of the other had their own consequences.

Yet, we might also note that there were many ways in which Jesus could have related the godliness or ungodliness of Dives (the rich man) and Lazarus (the poor man). Dives could have been an unfaithful husband and Lazarus a faithful one. Dives could have been a thief and Lazarus a trustworthy steward. And so on.

But again, Jesus chose to address the way wealth was used.

We should also be careful to note that there is not a shred of evidence that Dives had earned a penny in an unrighteous way or had failed to tithe. The godly management of wealth is about both righteous creation and graceful distribution.

Jesus said to his disciples, "Things that make people fall into sin are bound to happen, but how terrible for the one who makes them happen! It would be better for him if a large millstone were tied around his neck and he was thrown into the sea than for him to cause one of these little ones to sin. So watch what you do!"

(LUKE 17:1–3)

Jesus was realistic enough to know that sin happens. But, he was idealistic enough to know that it shouldn't be taught. So, modern evangelists should always take particular care to "watch what you do." Peter Wehner, the director of public policy at the conservative political think-tank Empower America, has wisely written:

> The New Testament says much more about the dangers of riches to one's soul than it does about many well-publicized issues about which many Christians feel so strongly. Yet you would never know this by the agenda advanced by America's most prominent and politically active Christian organizations, magazines and radio talk shows. . . . It's unwise for Christians to keep averting our gaze from warnings that Christ placed in bright neon lights. . . . In pursuit of wealth and worldly pleasures, Christians have become virtually indistinguishable from the rest of the world. We have bought into non-Christian precepts. Note the irony, Christians seeking and encouraging others to seek that which our Lord repeatedly warned against.

Not too long ago, a friend suggested that I had been too harsh in disagreeing with the economic concepts taught by a well-known Christian author and talk-show host. My friend said that at least the author had "discouraged materialism and encouraged giving." The irony is that the author is best known for having written several best-selling books about how bad the American economy is and will be in the future. So, while talking about America's materialism through a microphone in one hand, he was writing with the other that our economy wasn't producing enough material goods. And while the author did encourage giving to ministries, including his own, studies by groups such as Independent Sector were saying that economic pessimism of the sort shared by that same ministry was a major deterrent to charitable giving to colleges, churches, and the poor.

I take no delight in disagreeing with what my fellow Christians teach. Those who know me well will tell you that I try to get along with almost everybody. In fact, I find disagreeing most painful. Like most people, I like being liked. Perhaps too much. But, in both my vocation and avocation, I daily see evidence of how harmful such double-mindedness can be not only to the finances of people, but to their hearts, minds, and souls. And this scriptural text in Luke 17 about a millstone being hung around the necks of our teachers and leaders is serious enough that I am willing to risk discomfort—and probably a few friends—in order to save their souls.

There is also an economic dimension to the concept. There's an old Chinese proverb that says: "If you want one year of prosperity, grow grain. If you want ten years of prosperity, grow trees. If you want one hundred years of prosperity, grow people."

I would simply add that if you want one thousand years of prosperity, grow spirits.

Some Pharisees asked Jesus when the kingdom of God would come.
His answer was, "The kingdom of God does not come in such a way
as to be seen. No one will say, 'Look, here it is!' or, 'There it is!'
because the kingdom of God is within you."... "There will be those
who will say to you, 'Look, over there!' or, 'Look, over here!'
But don't go out looking for it."
(LUKE 17:20–23)

Many American Christians are looking for the physical return of Jesus and anticipating that he will establish his kingdom at any time. So-called end-times books can be described only as a publishing phenomenon. At the same time, sociologists tell us that there is very little difference between the hearts, souls, and minds of Christians and those of our secular neighbors. Are we looking outward when we should be looking inward? Might the physical kingdom develop more quickly if we focused our attentions "within," as Jesus suggested?

There is evidence it might. I once suggested that a friend should not hoard an expensive generator because of what she had been told about Y2K. I suggested she donate it instead to a Central American country that had been hard hit by a hurricane and whose needs were proven rather than speculative. But she was too filled with fear. So our fellow Christians in Central America went without power for heating and light. That's only one tiny example for how fear destroys the faith that might establish the kingdom.

It is also only one example of how many believe that Christianity and a sound economy are in tension. Many believe that preparation for Y2K was a major boost to the American economy since we replaced and repaired computers or laid in extra goods. That may have been true in the short run. But how do wasted generators benefit our economy in the long run? Could that be a reason the economy began weakening immediately after the millennium changed?

Might the world minimize such booms and busts by minimizing fear and greed?

Jesus also told this parable to people who were sure of their own
goodness and despised everybody else. "Once there were two men
who went up to the Temple to pray; one was a Pharisee, the other
a tax collector. The Pharisee stood apart by himself and prayed,
'I thank you, God, that I am not greedy, dishonest, or an adulterer,
like everybody else. I thank you that I am not like that
tax collector over there. I fast two days a week,
and I give you one tenth of all my income.'"

(LUKE 18:9–12)

I used to attend a lot of conferences on giving. Like most of those in attendance, I probably thought I was a better Christian because I gave to the various churches and ministries represented. And there were many times that
feeling was actually encouraged by those seeking donations.

Yet, the more I reflected on what Jesus had to say about such attitudes, the
more I realized I was only kidding myself. For Jesus taught that public religious acts such as fasting and tithing can blind us to the truth about ourselves. The tax collector was very conscious of how desperately he needed
God's grace. As a result, he was more likely to accept it, thereby "saving" his
heart, mind, and soul, not only for the next world but for this one.

That realization, which arrived far too late in my religious life, prompted
me to read a book with the unlikely title *God Hates Religion: How the Gospels
Condemn False Religious Practice*. It was written by Christopher Levan, a
Christian minister who observed:

> There is a hollow sentiment which passes for love; *the soul-destroying conde-
> scension of Christian charity*; and the pompous piety of the priestly. I cannot
> fail to notice the shallowness of faith that masquerades as devotion . . . I am
> constantly surprised by the Scriptures, or more precisely by the Christian
> Gospels; they too see the cracks in the smiling facade of religion; they too
> express a deep anger over ritualistic stupidity and blind piety that preens
> itself before the Lord. It could be that one of the central messages of the Bible
> is: "God hates that form of false religion." *(emphasis mine)*

There is man-made religion and there is religion integrated with the Loving Spirit of the Universe.

---

*Zacchaeus hurried down and welcomed Jesus with great joy.
All the people who saw it started grumbling, "This man has gone as
a guest to the home of a sinner!" Zacchaeus stood up and said to the
LORD, "Listen, sir! I will give half my belongings to the poor, and if
I have cheated anyone, I will pay him back four times as much."
Jesus said to him, "Salvation has come to this house today."*

(LUKE 19:6–9)

Not too long ago, *The Wall Street Journal* published a lengthy story about successful baby boomers returning to the church. Unfortunately, the article said the church didn't know how to respond to our renewed interest in spirituality.

So, how should the church and rich sinners approach one another? This story, so replete with symbolism, offers several suggestions.

1. Zacchaeus may have been the chief tax collector and rich, but the Bible tells us that he was still a "little man." Having been reminded too often about his lack of stature (a common story among many driven wealthy people that I meet), Zacchaeus thought he had to climb a tree to catch a glimpse of God. The first step to touching Ultimate Reality was actually for Zacchaeus to simply come down to earth.

2. Both we boomers and the church should expect many admirers of Jesus to grumble about our association. But, Jesus said he had very specifically come to "seek and save the lost"—and that includes wealthy sinners!

3. For Jesus and Zacchaeus, reconnecting was as simple as enjoying a meal together, which is always an act of friendship, even intimacy.

4. Zacchaeus truly repented of his past sins and gave evidence, with his money, of a new heart, mind, and soul toward the neighbors he had once looked down upon.

5. Finally, Jesus proclaimed that "Salvation has come to this house today." Not in the next world. Not at the Second Coming. Not after Zacchaeus had visited the church and been baptized. But *today*.

Of course, the people did not understand what Jesus was saying. The following verses tell us that "they supposed that the kingdom of God was just about to appear." But Jesus went on to tell the parable of the talents, which foretold his going away for a while.

Together, the parable of the talents and the salvation of Zacchaeus give us a balanced perspective of reality. While salvation may come to "this house" this very day and thereby assure a more abundant life, it may be a while before it comes to all houses, despite our well-intentioned hopes.

———————————————————— ❧ ————————————————————

Jesus looked around and saw rich men dropping their gifts
in the temple treasury, and he also saw a very poor widow dropping
in two little copper coins. He said, "I tell you that this poor widow
put in more than all the others. For the others offered their gifts
from what they had to spare of their riches; but she,
poor as she is, gave all she had to live on."

(LUKE 21:1–4)

Each of us has moments when we finally make connections that can change our worldviews in profound ways. This passage recently played a role in one such moment for me.

I had been invited to visit a friend named Isabelle Paul. Isabelle is a widow who was left quite well off when her husband passed away. Several years ago, she heard Robert Schuller remark how much he admired the story about the widow and her mites. She told him that she would like to tell the widow's story by placing her statue on the grounds of the Crystal Cathedral. So Isabelle commissioned the statue for the ministry. Upon its completion, the church unveiled it at a Sunday service, which was taped and broadcast. Isabelle had a copy and wanted me to see it since I had joined Dr. Schuller's board. After we watched it together, I told Isabelle that one of the very first things I have always hoped to do should I squeeze through that old eye of the needle is to spend a few minutes with the widow whom Jesus admired.

The following morning, I was to meet with some friends who were attending a Generous Giving conference being held at the Ritz Carlton in my hometown. One of my friends, a young Christian financial writer and stockbroker named Mary Naber, asked if she might spend the evening at our home since she couldn't afford the hotel. That evening, we began discussing my previous evening's activities with Isabelle. We realized that even though Jesus proclaimed the widow to be the most generous giver he had ever met, she had not given enough to get into many Christian conferences on giving. And she certainly couldn't have afforded the travel and hotel expense associated with such "generosity."

I'm not implying that there's anything wrong with us wealthy Christians getting together to discuss charitable trusts and foundations. But, can we really call ourselves "generous"? Might that simply be another form of pharisaic pride? And, by the standard Jesus established, aren't there far more people in the Third World who give "generously" than there are in America?

Jesus answered them, "My Father is always working,
and I too must work."
(JOHN 5:17)

Why does God go on working? After all, didn't God just create the world in six days and then start a very long nap, as suggested by Deists?

And, why did Jesus work during three long years of public ministry? If his only work was to die and be resurrected for the sins of the world, couldn't he have appeared and gotten that over with in a long weekend?

He never negotiated a large salary, as Ayn Rand might suggest, for so much "productive achievement." He never saved for retirement, as most of us might. But he worked so diligently that the Scriptures tell us that he often had to go away and rest.

The answer to those questions can shape our worldview, and our world, in profound ways, not only economically but theologically, politically, and spiritually as well. That worldview can then shape our activities, for better or worse.

When I was in a management development class on Wall Street, I listened as a manager explained that he liked to cut out pictures of expensive cars and tape them to brokers' phones. He thought that would motivate them to excel. I wondered if it wouldn't simply prompt the legal actions that typically follow aggressive sales tactics. Ultimately, it was that ethic that prompted me to turn more toward the church.

Ironically, I too often ran into the same ethic there. When I was thinking of attending seminary, I considered becoming an ordained lay minister of my denomination. That required several years of study, after which I would work in a voluntary capacity in the church. One of the first steps toward either goal was for my fellow lay leaders of the church to act as a board in assuring

I was headed in the right direction. I'll never forget that as I answered their questions, one of the leaders commented that she couldn't imagine why anyone would ever want to spend all that time studying and then work so hard when they weren't going to get paid for it. I realized then why the church has far fewer lay ministers than it might use.

I recall reading a book by David Stockman, the head of our government's office of management and budget during the Reagan years. The book was entitled *The Triumph of Politics*. Mr. Stockman was one of the very first to caution that the Reagan tax cuts and defense buildup during the 1980s would result in significant budget deficits. (He was also one of the first during the 1990s to say that the end of the Cold War would produce surpluses by the end of the decade.) Mr. Stockman told a story about why President Reagan was so insistent that the top tax brackets had to be cut substantially. It seems that when the President was an actor in Hollywood, his fellow stars would work until they reached the top tax bracket. They would then take the rest of the year off as their after-tax rewards weren't large enough to justify their efforts.

One can only wonder if our deficits and debt would have been smaller had the President's Hollywood friends worked out of love, in the image of God, rather than simply having worked for money in the image of Ayn Rand. Might the deficits and debt been smaller had Christians done the same?

------------------------------ ∽ ------------------------------

A third time Jesus said, "Simon, son of John, do you love me?" Peter became sad because Jesus asked him the third time, "Do you love me?" and so he said to him, "LORD, you know everything; you know that I love you!" Jesus said to him, "Feed my sheep."

(JOHN 21:17)

Only a few years ago, a secular and liberal newspaper writer referred to conservative Christians as less than scholarly and therefore easy to lead. Predictably, a furor arose in the conservative Christian media. You would have thought that the writer had called us sheep!

Naturally, the writer had used a less loving tone than the Good Shepherd. And many Christians might be correct when they equate "sheep" with the more innocent "lambs" from which sheep evolve. But this old farm boy has spent enough time with lambs, sheep, and people to wonder if Jesus didn't choose his words carefully.

Sheep are normally anything but the lovable creatures often depicted by painters, quietly being cuddled in the arms of the Good Shepherd. Like Jesus' disciples, sheep can stubbornly resist the best efforts of a good shepherd . . . but then blindly and loyally follow a smelly old goat—which is literally called a Judas Goat by slaughterhouse operators—to their deaths. Sheep are only the smartest animals in the pasture when they're the *only* animals in the pasture. And goodness knows how many times they are fleeced by someone interested in money.

I know that's a pretty humbling analogy. But a little more humility might make it easier for us to discern the lambs from the sheep . . . and goats!

THE TRUTH-FILLED, LOVING COMMUNITY OF THE EPISTLES

"A love which violates or even merely neutralizes truth is called by Luther, with his clear biblical vision, an 'accursed love,' even though it may present itself in the most pious dress. A love which embraces only the sphere of personal human relations and which capitulates before the objective and real can never be the love of the New Testament."

Dietrich Bonhoeffer, *Ethics*

The group of believers was one in mind and heart.
No one said that any of his belongings was his own,
but they all shared with one another everything they had.
With great power the apostles gave witness to the resurrection
of the LORD Jesus, and God poured rich blessings on them all.
There was no one in the group who was in need.

(ACTS 4:32)

THIS PASSAGE is often quoted by those who believe, as one famous theologian once put it, that "any serious Christian must be a socialist." Yet the text, as it appears in some modern translations, doesn't actually say that the early Christians held their possessions in common, which would be a primitive form of communism. (Some older translations do, so my point is not to deny that it does but to say there is some question about it.) Nor does it say that a government took what those possessions earned so it could be redistributed, which would be a form of socialism. It simply says the believers had experienced a change of heart, mind, and soul and were therefore willing to lovingly share what they had stewarded.

It also says, "God poured rich blessings on them all." We Americans should be careful about reading that through our cultural screens. Both biblical and nonbiblical evidence suggests that very few, much less "all" of the early Christians were what we might deem "rich" in a material sense. So the passage quite probably refers to great spiritual blessings and lesser material blessings. Yet, it is also quite clear that everyone had what they "needed," if not what they wanted or desired. That alone must have caused great joy among the group.

Later verses do tell us that the believers then sold what they owned and brought it to the leaders, who distributed it "to each according to his need." That meant the community was then left with essentially nothing to steward. Many theologians believe that was because the early church expected the imminent return of Jesus. Those same theologians believe that seeing the teachings of Jesus about his return from the short-term secular perspective of human beings rather than from the eternal perspective of God actually caused the economic depression in Jerusalem—the depression that the apostle Paul later sought to alleviate with his great collection for the early saints in Jerusalem.

So, from my perspective, the early community was neither communistic, socialistic, nor capitalistic, believing that private property is an absolute. It may have been something more like a transcendent version of "The Third Way" that Presidents Clinton and Bush, Prime Minister Tony Blair, and the London School of Economics have advocated in recent years. It might be described as *Religion and Liberty* described the worldview of Swiss economist Wilhelm Ropke: "When Ropke used the expression, 'third way,' he was emphasizing the need for a free society to complement the market economy and a limited state with both a flourishing range of intermediate associations as well as a moral culture that recognized what Christians understand as the objective hierarchy of values."

That is, the early community in Jerusalem was probably something quite similar to the Community of Jesus on Cape Cod. While some might disagree with parts of that group's theology, their stewardship approach might be closer to the New Testament church than anything I've run across.

I have made friends in that community who are quite wealthy. While they own their own home, which is quite large and comfortable, they make it available to visitors for short periods of time and to newcomers to the community for extended periods. There is almost never a time when another member of the community is not living there.

There are also common dormitories for those brothers and sisters at the Community who have taken vows of poverty. And, my family and I have been blessed by some of the most joyful meals in those dormitories we have ever shared with fellow Christians—including those meals we have had at the home of my wealthy friends. In short, each person there, whether resident or sojourner, prosperous or ascetic, has been richly blessed and no one is in need.

One day as we were going to the place of prayer, we were met by a slave girl who had an evil spirit that enabled her to predict the future. She earned a lot of money for her owners by telling fortunes. She followed Paul and us, shouting, "These men are servants of the Most High God! They announce to you how you can be saved!" She did this for many days, until Paul became so upset that he turned around and said to the spirit, "In the name of Jesus Christ I order you to come out of her!" The spirit went out that very moment. When her owners realized that their chance of making money was gone, they seized Paul and Silas and dragged them to the authorities in the public square.

(ACTS 16:16–19)

This passage is a clear warning that the ability to predict the future and speak about salvation does not automatically make one a prophet of God. Evil spirits can also speak through people, and even Satan can quote Scripture for his own purposes. It surely took considerable discernment on the part of Paul to recognize the slave girl's pronouncements as evil, for everything she said was true.

The Bible also shares the difficult reality that not everyone was happy Paul had driven the evil spirit away from the woman. There were men who were prospering quite nicely from her ability to predict the future even though it was from an evil source.

This passage might have been strangely relevant during the Y2K period. A very special but rather naive young woman had looked into the problem and decided it was going to be quite serious. She took her concerns to several male leaders who encouraged her to share her prophecies in a book, video, and seminars. Being young, she thought their interest validated her concern. But some of those leaders simply used her prophecies to sell books and tapes and to increase their influence over thousands of naive Christians. And as with the biblical account, not all of those leaders were happy when I tried to help the young woman understand what had happened to her.

I wish that were a rare and isolated example of women feeling used by men in the church. But it isn't. I'm particularly sensitive to those feelings because I have a widowed mother, two sisters, and a wife who may need the help of church leaders in the future. They should never need to fear that men will use them for money.

Everyone must obey state authorities, because no authority exists without God's permission, and the existing authorities have been put there by God. Whoever opposes the existing authority opposes what God has ordered; and anyone who does so will bring judgment on himself. . . . That is also why you pay taxes, because the authorities are working for God when they fulfill their duties. Pay then, what you owe them; pay them your personal and property taxes, and show respect and honor for them all.

(ROMANS 13:1–2,6–7)

Several years ago a woman saw me on Christian television and came to see me. She wanted my help in setting up what was called a medicaid trust. She was quite wealthy. But she wanted to become legally destitute. You see, if you put all your money in an irrevocable trust for your children, who can always give you what you really need, you can live off the government (that is, your neighbors who are paying taxes) for the rest of your life. Your children will not have to support you in your old age and will inherit more money. Unfortunately, they will also inherit a most unbiblical worldview.

I cited the Scripture above to the woman and explained gently but firmly why I thought her plan was immoral even though I have seen several of these prepared by "Christian attorneys" over the years. To say she was less than pleased by my counsel is an understatement, for she quickly began a series of "Yes, buts. . . ."

"Yes, but I already pay more than my fair share of taxes. Yes, but the government is wasteful. Yes, but the federal income tax is illegal. Yes, but the children of the inner cities live off the government." And so on.

I noted that she was very conservative theologically and asked if she really believed that human reason should overrule the Christian Scriptures. She replied that, of course, she didn't. She didn't appreciate it when I explained that she was making an exception to that belief by using her human reason to rationalize disobeying this passage. Naturally, the woman did not become a client. That didn't bother me, because deluded clients inevitably cause problems for advisors. But I was pained by the experience nonetheless.

We all rationalize our faith away from time to time, of course. But we may do it when the most is at stake, as Peter did the night before the crucifixion. Yet that is precisely when we have the opportunity to say the most to the world. So, whenever you're tempted to rationalize this passage away, reflect on these words from Billy Graham:

> I urge you not to cheat on your income tax . . . because you will be disobeying God. Furthermore, if you and other people fail to pay the taxes they owe, honest citizens will have to pay that much more just to make up the shortfall. I hope that you won't only resist the temptation to cheat on your taxes, but that you will stop and ask yourself why you would even consider it in the first place. Has money become too important to you? Are you allowing greed to rule you? Have you grown cynical about the government and those to whom God has entrusted the responsibility of leadership? Whatever the reason, don't let anything come before God and His will.

————————————— ✍ —————————————

I told you not to associate with immoral people. Now I did not mean
pagans. . . . To avoid them you would have to get out of the world
completely. What I meant was that you should not associate with
a person who calls himself a brother but is immoral or greedy. . . .
After all, it is none of my business to judge outsiders. God will judge
them. But should you not judge the members of your own fellowship?
(1 CORINTHIANS 5:9–13)

As you now know, I believe that if American Christianity had a problem during the 1990s, it was that we were quick to harshly judge our government officials, foreign officials, computer programmers, corporate leaders, and others, but equally quick to ignore the sins of our own religious leaders.

Many of my Christian friends in leadership positions believe I am wrong to associate no longer with those cultural judges who utilize our airwaves and publications to explain all that is wrong with others. Some believe I'm wrong to have turned back to working with Wall Street advisors who are ignorant of but interested in the true Christian ethic. Some believe I am wrong to write this book, which seems critical of the judges.

I simply pray that Paul had it right in the passage quoted above. For the future of our world might well depend on the moral leadership of America. That, in turn, depends on the moral leadership of the Christian church. And that, in turn, might depend on us understanding this passage from Paul.

All during the 1990s, prominent religious leaders told me privately that they did not believe what was being taught about the political economy in the Christian media. Yet, they also said they could never publicly contradict those teachings. During the Y2K fiasco I wrote to a friend who headed the National Religious Broadcasters about the need for an internal board to keep the religious "entrepreneurs" accountable. He replied that it wasn't practical but that he would publish an article about the media's excesses if I would write it. The irony of this was that even securities dealers have established a regulatory board, however fallible, to prevent the worst excesses of the industry. The other irony was that when Wall Street missed its prophecies less than the religious media did, investors filed many, many arbitration complaints against

Wall Street. But the media was protected by the constitution. And many Christians continued to worship religious media celebrities despite their selling a more distorted and impoverishing worldview than Wall Street did.

In the last several years, the Catholic Church has been under enormous pressure because its leaders did not feel they should publicly address their problems. As horrible as the private acts of sexual abuse by priests and resulting cover-ups might be, I'm not sure that God views them as any greater sins than broadcasting confusion, anger, and unbiblical teachings to God's masses while those who know better simply ignore it. The biblical ethic is that a sin is a sin, and one is no worse than another, as unfair as that seems and as uncomfortable as it makes us.

Christ asked us not to judge others. But, as Paul says, Jesus surely wants us to hold our fellow Christians accountable.

No one should be looking out for his own interests,
but for the interests of others.
(1 CORINTHIANS 10:24)

If I could define the difference between the Christian financial ethic and the "worldly" ethic, it would be this one sentence from Paul's first letter to the Corinthian church.

Notice that this counsel for altruism was stated not as a commandment but as a suggestion for a richer life. Paul used the word "should" rather than "must." Still, it is our selfless activities that bring joy and meaning to our lives, whether giving a present, feeding an abandoned cat, or making an anonymous donation.

The world economy can spin quite well if we simply obey the Great Commandment to consider our neighbors' interests as well as our own in all that we do. But it might continue to be more an efficient place to live than a spiritual place to live. So yes, practice ethics in all that you do. But as the bumper sticker says, leave some room in your schedule to "practice random acts of senseless kindness." Life will be richer for it. You will be happier for it.

Church leaders might also consider Paul's counsel in this Scripture.

Churches ask, quite legitimately, for the funds that pay staff salaries and advance ministry in the world, but those same churches also neglect the finances of their members by overlooking their member's needs and failing to teach the spiritual and moral dimensions of wealth management. No surprise then, that members wonder if church leaders are looking out for their own financial interests in contradiction to this counsel from Paul. He assured us that God will look out for our interests if we look out for the interests of others, as Moses and Jesus always did.

Each one should give, then, as he has decided, not with regret or out of a sense of duty; for God loves the one who gives gladly.

(2 CORINTHIANS 9:7)

As you know by now, this has not been a book focused primarily on giving. I have assumed that like most spiritual people, you have heard enough on that subject. But, that is not to slight giving in any way, for it remains one of the most enriching spiritual practices.

But frankly, I've grown quite disappointed at how often the first questions from Christians seem to be, "How much should I give? Should I tithe on my net income or my gross? Can I subtract the taxes I pay that go to the needy?" Each time I hear these kinds of questions I realize how little the church has explained the discipline of giving. I now ask, "How happy do you want to be?"

The only real additional guidance I might offer would be this counsel from C. S. Lewis, as found in *Mere Christianity*:

I do not believe one can settle how much we ought to give. I am afraid the only safe rule is to give more than we can spare. In other words, if our expenditure on comforts, luxuries, amusements, etc., is up to the standard common among those with the same income as our own, we are probably giving away too little. If our charities do not at all pinch or hamper us, I should say they are too small. There ought to be things we should like to do and cannot do because our charitable expenditure excludes them.

———————————— ✌ ————————————

You may be sure that no one who is immoral, indecent, or greedy
(for greed is a form of idolatry) will ever receive a share in the
Kingdom of Christ and of God.

(EPHESIANS 5:5)

During the 1990s, I worked with several ministries, including some financial ministries, that always seemed focused on the sins of government leaders, foreign governments, homosexuals, and others. Ironically, some seemed to exist solely for the purpose of helping their followers grow wealthier. Some even owed their personal wealth and the existence of their ministries to books and tapes that spiritually and materially impoverished the lives of their followers.

Few seemed to note that of all the sins Paul cautioned against, it was the sin of greed, or profiting at the expense of one's neighbor, that he singled out for special condemnation.

Perhaps capitalism, which is a religion and form of idolatry if it is not circumscribed by the moral order and spiritual freedom that transforms it into stewardship, has such a hold on our money culture that we will never be able to see that again. But for the sake of my son and my future grandchildren, I pray each morning that is not really true.

For the love of God, I hope you will as well.

———————————— ✌ ————————————

I urge you then, to make me completely happy by having the same
thoughts, sharing the same love, and being one in soul and mind.
Don't do anything from selfish ambition or from a cheap desire
to boast, but be humble toward one another, always considering
others better than yourselves. And look out for one
another's interests, not just for your own.

(PHILIPPIANS 2:2–4)

Several years ago, a small group of Lutheran pastors sued their pension board because it practiced biblical ethics in the management of money. It was basically the same ethic Sir John Templeton has adhered to over the decades; the same ethic that Sir John believes has actually enhanced his returns. But, the pastors thought the ethic would harm their returns. So, they wanted out of the fund.

The story was published widely in the financial press, earning full page status in *Barron's*. Frankly, it made sharing the Christian ethic on Wall Street quite difficult for some time. Several investors shared it as evidence Christians need not consider ethics. Several of my associates on Wall Street did the same.

And the apostle Paul surely shed a tear or two.

In conclusion my brothers, fill your minds with those things that are good and that deserve praise; things that are true, noble, right, pure, lovely, and honorable. Put into practice what you learned and received from me, both from my words and from my actions.

(PHILIPPIANS 4:8–9)

Like the apostle Paul, Sir John Templeton has some counsel for dealing with Wall Street analysts, politicians, the media, both secular and Christian, and others who want to fill your mind with negativity: Just don't listen!

Robert Bartley, the editor of *The Wall Street Journal,* adds that you also shouldn't *look* for the negativity. He has written on his op-ed page:

The new century, not unlike all other centuries, will provide plenty of reasons for pessimism if you start to look for them. But ultimately, pessimism is a snare and a delusion. Yes, there will be problems to confront, but there will also be opportunities to seize; in fact, the new century will be resplendent with opportunity.... We are still the richest society in the history of mankind. In the new century, we can, and should, choose optimism over pessimism. The danger of pessimism is that it is likely to be self-fulfilling.

Well said.

I know what it is to be in need and I know what it is to have more than enough. I have learned this secret, so that anywhere, at any time, I am content, whether I am full or hungry, whether I have too much or too little. I have the strength to face all conditions by the power that Christ gives me.

(PHILIPPIANS 4:12)

I expect that few readers of this book have too little resources, any more than many of you will be hungry. In fact, if you're like me, you probably need to shed a few pounds! And, you probably need to figure out what to do with your savings so they might honor God and serve your neighbor's interests as well as your own.

But like me, you may have a serious problem with being "content." Perhaps you want even more. Perhaps you are anxious that what you have is not enough. On the other hand, perhaps you already have so much that you believe it endangers your soul and the values of your children. Perhaps it was inherited and you are uneasy that it wasn't what the IRS terms "earned income." Perhaps . . .

I said in the opening pages of this book that one of my primary reasons for writing this book is so you might find the contentment that Paul experienced. I hope that by now you have either found that contentment or are, like me, further down the path toward it.

Using *all* your time, talent, and treasure for the glory of God and for the welfare of your neighbors as yourself is a glorious financial goal to strive for—perhaps the only one worthy of a spiritual investor practicing faithful finances.

Whatever you do, work at it with all your heart, as though you were working for the LORD and not for men.

(COLOSSIANS 3:23)

Jean-Pierre de Caussade once wrote in *The Joy of Full Surrender:*

> Just as fire warms us, rather than philosophical discussions about fire or knowledge of its effects, so the designs of God and His holy will work in the soul for its sanctification—not intellectual speculations concerning the principles or methods which produce holiness in our souls. When we are thirsty, we must drink: theoretical explanations will not quench our thirst. We must put speculation aside and drink in simplicity of all that the will of God sends us, both to do and to suffer.

Be confident that you have the basic intellectual tools for being a spiritual investor. It is now time to practice faithful finances.

Invest your time, talent, and treasure with all your heart. Do so with the passion of your soul. Do it for God. Not for me. Not for you. Not for your friends. Not for your boss. Not for your denomination. Not for your pastor. For God. Experience the fire that warms the heart.

———————————————— ✍ ————————————————

Whoever teaches a different doctrine and does not agree with the
true words of Jesus Christ and with the teaching of our religion
is swollen with pride and knows nothing. He has an unhealthy desire
to argue and quarrel about words, and this brings on insults, evil
suspicions, and constant arguments from people whose minds do not
function and who no longer have the truth. They think that religion
is a way to become rich. Well, religion does make a person very rich,
if he is satisfied with what he has. . . . For the love of money is
a source of all kinds of evil. Some have been so eager to have it
that they have wandered away from the faith and have broken
their hearts with many sorrows. But you, man of God,
avoid all these things. Strive for righteousness,
faith, love, endurance, and gentleness.
(1 TIMOTHY 6:3–10)

By now, I hope you understand the difference between "money" and "capital." Money, as it is typically criticized in the Bible, was simply currency of one nature or another that was being hoarded for one's own security or greed. But capital, as we understand it today, is not so much money as it is currency inspired with a creative spirit. It can be constructively creative or destructively creative. The first glorifies God by loving our neighbors as ourselves. The second loves only ourselves and, then, often for only the short-term.

During my career, I have been convinced that few Christians appreciate the facts about money. Even fewer appreciate such nuances about money as the difference between money and capital. And, almost no one appreciates the paradoxes of money. So you can be assured that many people will disagree with the perspectives of this book should you decide to share it with others.

The apostle Paul assures us that some of these critics will be Christians, perhaps Christian leaders. Perhaps they are right to disagree. I still know so very little.

You will now have to discern the truth for yourself. Filter these passages through the other hard teachings of the Scriptures. Use your head. Follow your heart. Hold to your soul. Work out your salvation with fear and trembling. Share your understanding of the truth with patience, gentleness, and grace. Forgive me when I have not. I have erred out of love.

Each one, as a good manager of God's different gifts, must use for
the good of others the special gift he has received from God.
(1 PETER 4:10)

The Wall Street Journal once observed how a nonbiblical theology of work affects our world. It commented:

> The persistent message coming from the pulpit stresses the importance of being "called" to the "full-time ministry." The only people who are doing "God's work" are evangelists, teachers and the like. Such non-ministers as carpenters *[note the irony there]*, housewives, doctors and politicians, when they become Pentecostals, risk being second-class citizens in the "Kingdom of God." If there is no future (the world's end is imminent), why bother with these "temporal" pursuits?

You have been given a special gift. It is different from mine. It is different from God's gifts to others. It is different than your pastor's. They need your gift, as do I. Use it well. Use it as Peter advised in the Scripture above, not as humans advise.

―――――――――――――――― ✍ ――――――――――――――――

If a rich person sees his brother in need, yet closes his heart against
his brother, how can he claim that he loves God? My children,
our love should not be just words and talk;
it must be true love, which shows itself in action.

(1 JOHN 3:17)

To this point, I have been rather critical of the mass media. But, the wonder of television has done one thing for a rich America. It has allowed us to see our neighbors in need as never before. Some say that has simply given us "compassion fatigue" and further hardened our hearts. I hope not.

America has far more than we need. Not only do we have the two coats that Jesus referred to, but most of us have two homes, two cars, two televisions, and two or more of lots of others things. That is both a challenge and an opportunity. We can spend this century growing even richer but more mentally and spiritually ill. Or, we can embark on a millennium of meaning by sharing our vast material and financial riches, as well as our more limited spiritual riches of heart, soul, and mind, with those in need. Better still, we can help them to create their own riches by investing in their dreams and graciously accepting their bountiful spiritual gifts.

Yes, it's all right to talk about our beliefs. But, let's remember that ours is "true love" only when we act on those beliefs. So, even though I have disagreed often with the economic and political worldview shared by Focus On The Family, I do hope you'll remember these words of Dr. James Dobson, who has always been and will always be a devoted and beloved child of our God:

I am concerned that when it comes to money and material things, we live as if there is no eternity and no hope of the coming of Jesus. We are self-indulgent and hoard our resources for our own benefit rather than investing them for kingdom purposes. [Again, I would disagree if Dr. Dobson is implying that we should give *everything* to ministries rather than productive commercial and public enterprises but I don't think that's what he meant.] We believe in the Second Coming. We believe that our stewardship will be judged. But we actually live as if God did not exist and Jesus was in fact not coming. I would say that makes us eschatological atheists.

Or, as Father John Haughey, one of the most learned teachers about money in our culture, said: "We read the Gospel as if we had no money; and we spend our money as if we know nothing of the Gospel."

Believe in God's love. Act in God's love. Invest in God's love.

--------- ℘ ---------

There is no fear in love: perfect love drives out all fear.
So then, love has not been made perfect in anyone who is afraid.
(1 JOHN 4:18)

As the last millennium neared its end, *The Economist* published an article entitled "Sam, Sam, The Paranoid Man." It said: "When Americans look at their economy these days, they are horrified by what they see, or think they see. Economist paranoia has become an American habit."

As I write, America has been through yet another recession. It is one of the lightest the world has seen since the seven lean years of Egypt. But of course, pessimistic pundits of all stripes believe it is a sign that the end is near. Perhaps it is. But maybe it's not.

As you decide whom to believe, it might enrich you spiritually to remember that media critic Michael Medved has spoken these words at Hillview College:

In recent years, our nation has been torn by fears. . . . This depressed and nihilistic attitude toward life could be the biggest threat to America today. . . . Human beings will not learn, will not grow, and will not develop good character traits if they believe that discipline and hard work are pointless, that life is meaningless and unfair, and that the outlook for the future is grim.

It might also enrich you financially to remember that Sir John Templeton and I believe the Dow will reach the 1 million level later this century, God willing.

God's love can make that a reality, regardless of the pessimism of human beings. The only thing we have to fear truly is fear (and maybe greed) itself. There is no fear in love.

Part IV

The Loving Spirit of True Wealth Creation

~

"The West must find a way of putting individual initiative, the necessary driving-force of progress, within a shaping moral order. . . . Otherwise, the history books will record that the people of the West woke up during the 21st century to discover that the pursuit of efficiency was not the same as the achievement of a happy life. The West, they will say, found itself living in a superbly efficient but, in the end, aimless machine."

The Economist

CHAPTER NINE

A VISION FOR THE THIRD
MILLENNIUM

"The individual needs to return to spiritual values, for he can survive in the present human situation only by reaffirming that man is not just a biological and psychological being but also a spiritual being, that is creature, and existing for purposes of his Creator and subject to Him."

Peter Drucker, *Landmarks of Tomorrow*

"There is an important distinction to be made between what we might call ethical and spiritual acts. An ethical act is one where we refrain from causing harm to others' experience or expectation of happiness. Spiritual acts we can describe in terms of those qualities such as love, compassion, patience, forgiveness, humility, tolerance, and so on which presume some level of concern for others' well-being. We find that the spiritual actions we undertake which are motivated not by narrow self-interest but out of concern for others actually benefit ourselves. And they make our lives meaningful."

The Dalai Lama, in *Ethics for the New Millennium*

"We always felt that we were doing good—not only for our investors, helping them to make more profits—but also for the nations where we invested. If we send money to buy shares in corporations in the poverty stricken nations, then those corporations can expand more readily and help people. Furthermore, most of those poor nations need infrastructure, such as more pure water, or more telephones, or more highways, and you can't do that by local savings. So you need to have the foreigners to come in and buy shares in order that your infrastructure can be the foundations of the entrepreneurship among the local people."

Sir John M. Templeton, as quoted in
Ten Golden Rules for Financial Success by Gary Moore

I adapted the following from a talk I gave for the Making a Profit While Making a Difference Conference held May 10-12, 2000, ironically at the World Trade Center in New York City. It was a meeting of ethical, but not necessarily spiritual, institutional investors. When contemplating how to begin, I knew many of them would embrace the words of the Dalai Lama but block the words of Jesus Christ, even if they were the same words. Conversely, some reviewers of this book have blocked the Dalai Lama's words simply because they are from the Dalai Lama and not Christ. While I "have become all things to all men for the sake of Christ," I still long for a world where we not only listen to each other, but love each other.

A s we begin a new millennium, most investors and laborers remain content simply to receive a return of more money on the money and/or time and talent they invest, which might be a good definition of Western-style capitalism. But during recent decades, the West may have begun what Dr. Peter Drucker calls the "post-capitalist society," where both investors and laborers have sought a social return as well. Those ethical, socially responsible, or values-based investors have typically sought a double bottom line. Yet, much of the consciousness about social investing has still been about simply avoiding investments in potentially harmful endeavors, such as the so-called sin stocks of alcohol, tobacco, and gambling companies, and a few variations, such as media companies promoting non-spiritual values and Enron-style corporations practicing irresponsible accounting.

But the exploding popularity of books on spirituality, such as the bestseller by the Dalai Lama cited above, may indicate that more of us in the West are increasingly seeking spiritual returns as well, though not at the possible expense of financial gain. Yet we too should look back after a financially successful career and still say, as Sir John Templeton did, "We always felt that we were doing good. . . ." Not just avoiding harm but doing good. Not just with charitable dollars that are a small percentage of our incomes—as my religious clients are essentially taught year after year by our religious institutions—but with our principal as well. Not guided by fear or greed but by love.

The irony of today's consciousness is that Jewish patriarchs were among the earliest advocates of spiritual investing. Please review Exodus 21:28–33,

Leviticus 19:9, Deuteronomy 15:9, and Deuteronomy 22:8 for only a few examples of the patriarchs' "do good" teachings that encouraged social investing and other activities beyond charitable giving. This higher dimension keeps wealth managers connected to the gracious Creative Spirit and therefore to the souls of we the created, and is common to many spiritual traditions. For example, two central teachings of the Christian tradition are that humankind cannot live by bread alone, though Christ chose it along with wine to represent his very being, and that the truly abundant life has two dimensions beyond material well-being: the horizontal or social dimension and the vertical or spiritual dimension. That's only one belief about reality that is expressed by our symbolic cross, but it is a most important one. The implication is that the truest riches are threefold: a triple bottom line of financial, social, and spiritual returns.

The peace that I have often found in the offices of Sir John Templeton, who is perhaps the most spiritual of the Wall Street legends, is not unlike that I often find in a chapel. The joy I've often seen in his face is not unlike the joy I've often seen in the faces of the Dalai Lama and Christian monks. I believe such joy affirms that triple rewards are not only *possible* for successful investors but that they may be complementary. If you'll excuse a personal example, let me share an experience that speaks volumes about this conclusion.

Just after the developing markets of Southeast Asia suffered a sharp decline during 1998, the November issue of *Money* featured an article about spiritually oriented investment advisors. During an interview for that article, I mentioned that most Americans were heading for treasury securities but some of my friends, clients, and I were headed increasingly for Southeast Asia by doubling our investments in those markets. I shared with the interviewer that we were particularly fond of South Korea, which happens to be the home of the largest Christian church in the world. And I explained that by investing there, we were simply following the spiritual principle of loving our neighbors as ourselves. *Money* wrote that I was a believer who takes the idea of spiritual investing to "unexpected lengths." I might have been tempted by that old sin of religious pride had the writer's tone not been that we had just taken the financial equivalent of a long walk off a short pier!

A year later, the good news was that the developing markets funds were among 1999's best-performing assets. The South Korean market more than doubled. And a crisis that President Clinton called one of the greatest threats to America's economy since the Great Depression passed without permanent damage. Perhaps that is why Peter Drucker has also emphasized: "The developed countries also have a tremendous stake in the Third World. Unless there is rapid development there—both economic and social—the developed countries will be inundated by a human flood of Third World immigrants far beyond their economic, social or cultural capacity to absorb."

This "harmony of interests," as Adam Smith called it, was once noted by *The Economist*. It made the case that Mark Mobius, the manager of the various Templeton developing markets funds, had not only compiled a ten-year track record virtually identical to the vaunted S&P 500 index but that he has "almost certainly" done more good for the world's poor than Mother Teresa. From a spiritual perspective, that conclusion is surely open to debate, particularly if we consider how Mother Teresa enriched the spiritually poor of the materially rich nations, myself included. But from an economic perspective, it surely contains more than an element of truth. While Mother Teresa admirably consoled the destitute, Mark has just as admirably sought to prevent others from becoming destitute.

I am both an investment advisor and board treasurer of a "microcredit" ministry that finances tiny jobs for that fifth of humanity who live on less than $1 per day. We finance them by raising charitable donations and then making loans that average about $200 each. I am constantly amazed at how the traditional capital markets of the U.S.—long estimated at well over $30 trillion—dwarf the alternative capital markets. Mark Mobius alone manages more than $13 billion. But $100 million is a significant sum in the microcredit world. Both the developed and the developing worlds would surely be more hopeful, peaceful, and prosperous places if only 1 percent of the traditional markets found its way into developing markets funds and microcredit organizations. Another 1 percent in "community development" institutions such as Chicago's South Shore Bank might work miracles among the materially disadvantaged in the U.S.

But spiritual investing may influence far more than the sheer size of the traditional markets. As "chaos theory" intimates, markets that are motivated by fear and greed can do harm to the most vulnerable in indirect ways. For example, as the new millennium began, *The Wall Street Journal* observed:

Conventional wisdom holds that the Federal Reserve's five recent interest-rate increases are having little effect on the surging U.S. economy, including the rate-sensitive housing sector. But beneath the radar screen of many government statisticians, developers of low- and moderate-income housing say the rate increases are exacerbating a near crisis in the affordable housing market, forcing the delay or cancellation of thousands of projects.

It was commonly assumed that speculation in the technology-stock dominated Nasdaq, which made a most irrational run to the 5000 level, was a major factor for the rate increases as the Federal Reserve sought to cool the speculative fires. The God who brings order out of chaos could have made those increases unnecessary.

Noting this makes us as popular as John Bogle, the thrift-obsessed founder of the Vanguard Funds, at a load-fund convention. But, some spiritual leaders wonder if even social investors should heavily over-weight U.S. technology companies, "clean" though they might be, particularly when technology companies typically sell at far more reasonable valuations in international markets. For example, Professor Freeman Dyson won the Templeton Prize for Progress in Religion, which was founded by Sir John to be the spiritual equivalent of the Nobel Prizes, as the new millennium began. The press release described Professor Dyson as "one of the world's preeminent physicists whose futurist views consistently challenge humankind to reconcile technology and social justice." It added that this spiritual "man of a third culture in the making," meaning he transcends the "liberal/conservative" labels, has "chastised science for concentrating too much technology in 'making toys for the rich'—cellular phones, ever-smaller laptop computers, and the like—rather than helping to spread knowledge, well-being, and wealth around the world so that one day 'every Egyptian village can be as wealthy as Princeton.'" As more than two-thirds of the world's homes did not have a telephone as the old millennium came to a close, we essentially wonder how much capital can be morally devoted to "toys."

Yet, be not afraid that spiritual investing must enrich our neighbors at our expense. When Sir John Templeton last graced the cover of *Forbes*, he said the way for investors to beat the market over the long term was to invest at his famous "point of maximum pessimism." Our investment in South

Korea was only one example of how having "faith" when others had lost hope has enriched our shareholders. That faith during a time of trouble has been a characteristic of spiritual investors since Jeremiah bought his field in a time of pending crisis (see Jeremiah 32).

The corollary to Sir John's maxim is to sell before the point of maximum euphoria, or greed. That too has social and spiritual dimensions. During the late 1980s, Sir John suggested that Japan would be wise to invest its excess capital in other nations rather than to bid up Japan's stocks, bonds, and real estate to speculative levels. Few were humble enough (humility being a prime spiritual discipline!) to listen. He was even criticized in a 1992 *Forbes* cover story for leaving the Japanese party too early. But, then the hangover arrived. And when the price/earnings ratio—which we believe remains a useful if imperfect tool for measuring capital utilization—of America's Nasdaq 100 soared to levels not even seen in Japan, we redirected our capital since not only was the need greater elsewhere, the risks to our capital, and spirits, were lower as well. As the medieval monk described the eternal cycle: Discipline creates abundance, abundance destroys discipline, and discipline, in its fall, destroys abundance.

The recent past suggests a more patient spirit might also enrich us during the coming millennium. The January 15, 2000, issue of *The New York Times* said that investors were only holding stocks for eight months on average as the old millennium gave way to the new. They held Nasdaq stocks just five months on average and held the fifty Nasdaq stocks with the heaviest trading for just three weeks on average. Meanwhile, mutual fund managers have been trading all our stocks about each year on average. But Mr. Bogle found in studies done at Vanguard that there is a strong but inverse relationship between trading and returns. During his career, Sir John held his stocks about five years, about the length of a typical business cycle. Warren Buffett has always said his favorite holding period is "forever." Both are closer to the eternal perspective advocated by many spiritual traditions. Socially, it's doubtful that rapid-fire traders bother with corporate governance issues and so on. Spiritually, trading seems a most stressful way to manage wealth.

People sitting in a casino hour after hour rarely appear particularly joyful. It seems little different with rapid-fire traders, whether on our exchanges, in our day-trading firms, on the Internet, or in Silicon Valley. The spiritual poverty that has accompanied the quick wealth of the Valley was recently the subject of a feature article in *Money*. Entitled "Heal the Rich!," the article's headline read: "So you dreamed that wealth would bring you happiness? Think again. Newly minted millionaires now flock to shrinks, seeking a cure for the latest psychiatric malady: 'Sudden-Wealth syndrome.'"

In short, Christ never condemned wealth; but he knew that we might condemn our minds and spirits in its pursuit. So he asked us to always add the ethical and spiritual dimensions to our investing as not only would they put more bread into the mouths of our neighbors, they would put more peace in our souls and joy on our faces.

As we journey further into our new millennium, understanding why this integration of ethics and spirit is Judeo-Christian (and I assume Buddhist, Taoist, and Hindu) might help us to better understand our more integrated Muslim cousins. That might, in turn, be a major investment in world peace and prosperity. For it might help the rest of the world to see us not as ugly Americans selling materialism, sex, and violence but as beautiful Christians giving spirituality, brotherhood, and love.

God *has* blessed America. Now let *us* bless the world.

Recommended Reading

Some books may be out of print but may be available from Amazon.com.

Albion, Mark. *Making a Life, Making a Living: Reclaiming Your Purpose and Passion in Business and in Life.* New York: Warner Books, 2000.

Arterburn, Stephen, and Jack Felton. *Toxic Faith: Experiencing Healing over Painful Spiritual Abuse.* Colorado Springs: Harold Shaw Publishers, 2001.

Bakker, Jim. *Prosperity and the Coming Apocalypse.* Nashville: Thomas Nelson, 1998.

Berger, Peter L. *The Capitalist Revolution: Fifty Propositions About Prosperity, Equality, and Liberty.* New York: Basic Books, 1986.

Berger, Peter L. *The Capitalist Spirit: Toward a Religious Ethic of Wealth Creation.* Oakland, Calif.: ICS Press, 1990.

Berryessa, Norman, and Eric Kirzner. *Global Investing: The Templeton Way.* New York: McGraw-Hill Trade, 1992.

Bonhoeffer, Dietrich. *Ethics.* New York: Touchstone Books, 1995.

Colson, Charles W., and Nancy Pearcy. *How Now Shall We Live?* Grand Rapids, Mich.: Zondervan, 2000.

Crane, Christopher A., and Mike Hamel. *Executive Influence: Impacting Your Workplace for Christ.* Colorado Springs: NavPress Publishing Group, 2003.

Dalai Lama. *Ethics for the New Millennium.* New York: Riverhead Books, 2001.

Drucker, Peter F. *Post-Capitalist Society.* New York: Harper Business, 1994.

Fogel, Robert. *The Fourth Great Awakening and the Future of Egalitarianism: The Political Realignment of the 1990s and the Fate of Egalitarianism.* Chicago: University of Chicago Press, 2000.

Gonzalez, Justo. *Faith and Wealth: A History of Early Christian Ideas on the Origin, Significance, and Use of Money.* Eugene, Oreg.: Wipf & Stock Publishers, 2002.

Lederach, Paul M. *A Third Way: Conversations About Anabaptist/Mennonite Faith.* Scottdale, Pa.: Herald Press, 1980.

McKay, Charles. *Extraordinary Popular Delusions and the Madness of Crowds.* Philadelphia: Templeton Foundation Press, 1999 [original 1841].

Merton, Thomas. *No Man Is an Island.* San Diego: Harvest Books, 2002.

Moore, Gary. *Spiritual Investments: Wall Street Wisdom from the Career of Sir John Templeton.* Philadelphia: Templeton Foundation Press, 1998.

Myers, Bryant L. *Walking with the Poor: Principles and Practice of Transformational Development.* Maryknoll, N.Y.: Orbis Books, 1999.

Nash, Laura L. *Church on Sunday, Work on Monday: The Challenge of Fusing Christian Values with Business Life.* Somerset, N.J.: Jossey-Bass, 2001.

Nasr, Seyyed Hossein. *The Heart of Islam: Enduring Values for Humanity.* San Francisco: HarperSanFrancisco, 2002.

Needleman, Jacob. *Money and the Meaning of Life.* New York: Doubleday Publishing, 1994.

Neuhaus, Richard John. *Doing Well and Doing Good: The Challenge to the Christian Capitalist.* New York: Doubleday Publishing, 1992.

Nouwen, Henri J. M. *Lifesigns: Intimacy, Fecundity, and Ecstasy in Christian Perspective.* New York: Doubleday Publishing, 1989.

Novak, Michael. *Business as a Calling: Work and the Examined Life.* New York: Free Press, 1996.

Novak, Michael. *The Spirit of Democratic Capitalism.* New York: Madison Books, 1991.

O'Hear, Anthony. *After Progress: Finding the Old Way Forward.* New York: Bloomsbury Publishing, 2000.

Opitz, Edmund A. *Religion and Capitalism: Allies, Not Enemies.* Irvington-on-Hudson, N.Y.: Foundation for Economic Education, 1992.

Rae, Scott, and Kenman Wong. *Beyond Integrity: A Judeo-Christian Approach to Business Ethics.* Grand Rapids, Mich.: Zondervan, 1996.

Robbins, John W. *Without a Prayer: Ayn Rand and the Close of Her System.* Unicoi, Tenn.: Trinity Foundation, 1997.

Schaeffer, Francis A. *A Christian Manifesto.* Wheaton, Ill.: Crossway Books, 1981.

Seligman, Martin E. P. *Authentic Happiness: Using the New Positive Psychology to Realize Your Potential for Lasting Fulfillment.* New York: Free Press, 2002.

Templeton, John Marks. *Worldwide Laws of Life.* Philadelphia: Templeton Foundation Press, 1997.

Wallis, Jim. *The Soul of Politics: Beyond "Religious Right" and "Secular Left."* San Diego: Harcourt Trade Publishers, 1995.

Weber, Max. *The Protestant Ethic and the Spirit of Capitalism.* New York: Dover Publications, 2003.

Wuthnow, Robert. *God and Mammon in America.* New York: Free Press, 1994.

Subject and Name Index

Scripture Index